L. W. Marks
A Baptist Progressive in Missouri & Oklahoma
1862-1943

To L. W. "Whit" Marks III whose example gave me the principal foundation for my personal and professional growth, encouraging the merger of faith, practice and scholarship.

ISBN-13: 978-0-9801084-3-3

MONGREL EMPIRE PRESS
NORMAN, OKLAHOMA, UNITED STATES OF AMERICA

WWW.MONGRELEMPIREPRESS.COM

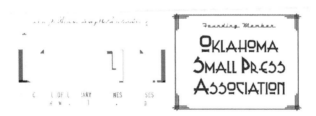

Founding Member

OKLAHOMA
SMALL PRESS
ASSOCIATION

All photographs & ephemera courtesy of L. W. Marks III

Cover: *L. W. Marks, his "wheel," and the roads he traveled.*
© JLC Mish, 2009

Book Design: Mongrel Empire Press using iWork Pages.

L. W. Marks

A Baptist Progressive in Missouri & Oklahoma
1862-1943

By

Alvin O. Turner

Foreword by
Jerry L. Faught II

MONGREL EMPIRE PRESS NORMAN, OK

Table Of Contents

Foreword

Individuals familiar with the history of Edmond, Oklahoma and those who are acquainted with early Oklahoma Baptist history will recognize the name L.W. Marks (1862-1943). Marks made a name for himself as civic leader in Edmond and as a pastor and denominational leader among Oklahoma Baptists. He may be best known as the father of Oklahoma Baptist historians although during his day he received little recognition for his work. Nevertheless, all subsequent Oklahoma Baptist historians stand on his shoulders. Although Marks is certainly a person worthy of study, surprisingly, no detailed treatment of Marks's life has appeared—until now.

Alvin O. Turner, long time university administrator, history professor, and noted authority on Oklahoma history, has written a superb biography of this significant but neglected Oklahoma figure. Turner's research is impressive as he has consulted numerous primary sources and interpreted them fairly. Turner does not lionize and gloss over Marks's weaknesses or his failings as is the temptation for any biographer writing about an admirable personality. Turner presents Marks's virtues as well as his flaws. According to Turner, Marks was a devoted churchman and family man who had many interests and tackled his work with great energy but frequently did not achieve the success for which he longed. Although Turner's treatment of Marks is balanced and impartial, in no way is the work nondescript. Turner's provocative thesis, which he argues convincingly, is that Marks can be best understood as a Baptist progressive having been influenced primarily by that force while a student at Southern Seminary where the progressive spirit flourished at the time. Certainly, Marks did not represent progressive ideals fully, but as Turner suggests, Marks advanced some of the causes associated with the progressive era and sought to influence Baptists in Oklahoma to do the same.

The various causes Marks championed included associational cooperation, Baptist higher education, an educated ministry, a fair and balanced denominational newspaper, missions, Sunday School work, and various social issues such as temperance. He did all this while serving primarily as a busy pastor and denominational leader. Marks challenged Oklahoma Baptists to put away a narrow focus and the provincialism that characterized much of Baptist life in Oklahoma at the turn of the twentieth century and embrace a larger vision. Unfortunately, Marks did not achieve his goals as the two principal agencies that he promoted as a means of reaching his aims, Oklahoma Baptist College and Word and Way Baptist newspaper, never found a noteworthy place among Oklahoma Baptists. Turner demonstrates that Marks not only failed to accomplish these goals, but he also experienced financial setbacks as a businessman, and suffered the death of his daughter Zulah. According to Turner, however, Marks should not be viewed as a tragic figure but as an indefatigable person who in the face of disappointment and broken dreams remained active in various Baptist and community causes until his death.

Alvin Turner has rendered exceptional service for Oklahomans in general and Oklahoma Baptists in particular by uncovering the life of one of their important early leaders. Baptists today would do well to revisit Marks and reflect upon his emphases. While Baptists in the state may have taken up some aspects of his agenda, an enduring and crippling parochialism remains.

JERRY L. FAUGHT II
Dickinson Associate Professor of Religion
Oklahoma Baptist University
President, Baptist History and Heritage Society 2007-2009

Acknowledgments

Completing even the smallest research and writing project always requires the assistance of numerous others. In this instance, the book could not have been completed without the support of the Marks family. An interview with L.W. Marks' two surviving children was crucial to gaining insight to the impact of his ministry on his children. Materials compiled by L. W. Marks III including those in his possession and those he had earlier worked to place in the Gaskin Archives of the Oklahoma Baptist Historical Society represented the foundation for the story I was able to tell and one I could not have completed without those materials. I also benefitted greatly from his encouragement and criticism as well as that of Charles F. "Freddie" Marks whose genealogical and other research allowed me to place L. W. Marks' story in the larger contexts of Marks family, frontier, and Baptist history. Freddie is also involved in a project to bring L. W. Marks' diaries to print, thereby increasing access to the thoughts and contributions of that remarkable man.

As this effort was delayed for more than ten years by a career move that did not permit the sustained attention required for a book, I also acquired long term debts to Angela Stiffler, the archivist at William Jewell College and a succession of secretaries of the Oklahoma Baptist

Historical Commission and others who have worked with the Commission archives during the past decades. Especially important were Eli Sheldon, the current historical secretary, and Dr. J. M. Gaskin, the principal founder of the commission and the person most responsible for its strengths and those of the Oklahoma Baptist Archives. Gaskin has also written more on Oklahoma Baptist history than any other person and his studies provided a significant foundation for mine as it has for others. He rightly labeled L.W. Marks as the "stackpole" for Oklahoma Baptist historians but Gaskin has been the one who has done the majority of the stacking during the twentieth century. He also offered valuable advice as well as encouragement in the early stages of my research.

I also need to acknowledge the assistance given by Paulette Orahood of the Barton County Missouri Historical Society. Her dedicated work to answer a question about a small part of my chapter on Marks years in Lamar, Missouri added to my account but also reminded me of the valuable work being done by volunteers in countless historical endeavors preserving vital pieces of the larger national narrative.

Finally, both Jerry Faught and Carole Joyce assisted with editing and I have to thank Sarah Garcia one more time. Her agreement to help with the typing is the only reason this manuscript was completed this year.

Introduction

Luther Whitfield (L. W.) Marks was a progressive Baptist pastor, denominational leader, newspaperman, historian, community leader, and businessman in Missouri and Oklahoma. As a Baptist leader, he called for a central organization to foster cooperation among all of the Baptists in a region, a school of higher learning for the education of their children, and a denominational paper of general circulation. Arguing that Baptists get "lopsided" when they lacked such institutions, he asserted that:

> Without the first, through which we may combine and direct our efforts, our resources and strengths go to waste. Without the second, the young life coming into our churches remains undeveloped and untrained for our particular work. Without the third, we have no certain knowledge of how the battle goes from day to day, and our great campaign to conquer the world degenerates into a guerilla warfare, only irritating and angering the enemy. [1]

Marks' impact was especially noteworthy in Oklahoma where he was a key figure in establishing modern Baptist work during two periods as agent-editor for the Missouri-based *Word & Way*, 1903-1906 and 1909 1911. Ultimately, his leadership in that capacity and other roles helped define Baptist higher education, social services and newspapers in the new state. His work as a denominational historian was also notable, earning him recognition as the "father of Oklahoma Baptist historians," the "stackpole"[2] for those who succeeded him as preservers and recorders of the denominational past.

Before those accomplishments, he completed his education at Southern Seminary in 1897, pastored churches in Missouri, and directed associational work in the Wyaconda Association. He concluded his full-time ministry in Edmond, Oklahoma. He served that town as mayor from 1913-1915 and on the city council from 1919-1924 during which time he also established one of the community's landmark businesses.

He wrote regular diary entries from 1898, and the beginning of his studies at Southern Seminary, until 1918. The earliest entries have special interest because he was a first-hand observer of the denomination-wide conflict that surrounded William H. Whitsitt's tenure as seminary president. Marks' perceptions of the president and the conflicts surrounding his administration add to that story as well as providing a picture of seminary life at the time. Later entries permit similar insight into aspects of a small town pastor's life; a reform movement in Lamar, Missouri; politics in Edmond, Oklahoma; and the growth of Oklahoma Baptist work. The travel he completed for the *Word & Way*, his longtime work with associations, and his writing on numerous state issues provide a rich supplement to any understanding of that growth.

Linking Marks' commitments by reference to the progressive era that shaped American political and cultural life in the first decades of the twentieth century places his career in context but also creates numerous problems. The progressives are usually identified with a wide variety of state and national political reforms. The movement also promoted civic improvements but had their most noticeable impact on the larger cities. In fact, the reformers were not defined by a cohesive agenda or direction as much as they were by shared assumptions and values. These included a conscious response to modernization with a corresponding commitment to changes to promote efficiency, cooperation, education and similar responses.

Baptists are not usually thought of as progressive, and Marks' goals might not be recognized by many as consistent with that movement. There is a broad-based failure to recognize the historical complexity of Baptists generally and Southern Baptists in particular. They are usually depicted as being composed of small town and rural congregations, defined by a narrow focus, and limited material and educational resources through most of the nineteenth and much of the twentieth century. Much of that definition is factual but there were numerous and significant exceptions to the rule from the faculty at Southern Seminary to pastors of large urban churches and even at churches throughout the Wyaconda Baptist Association of Missouri, the First Baptist Churches of Lamar, Missouri and of Edmond, Oklahoma when L. W. Marks served as their pastor. Even more to the point, the truthful aspects of that picture of Southern Baptist provincialism defined the progressive agenda among denominational advocates for reform such as Marks.

Marks' calls for expanded cooperation, higher education and a reliable denominational newspaper specifically addressed the roots of provincialism among those he referred to as lopsided Baptists. For Marks, such Baptists were those defined by some narrow interest or favored teaching that dominated the proclamations of the good news. Their limited focus also meant that they rarely looked outside of their own immediate concerns to address the larger issues of society. They were, however, entrenched at every level of Baptist life and the source for many of the struggles and disappointments he would face throughout his ministry.

The moral flavor of the civic reform goals he worked toward as a civic leader in Lamar, Missouri and Edmond, Oklahoma could cause yet others to question his progressive credentials. The deep religious roots of progressivism are ignored by many historians, while those who study its religious aspects are prone to focus on their development within those denominations now identified as mainstream. This interpretive dilemma becomes even more problematic among contemporary Southern Baptists who may wrongly equate the term progressive with either a discredited liberalism or as the name for a group that has opposed convention leadership during the past three decades.[3]

Numerous interrelated historical problems add to the resultant interpretive confusion and conflicts. The first problem arises from fundamental disagreements among historians about what progressivism was and even if such a movement existed.[4] That issue exacerbates the conflicts many historians face who are uncomfortable with religious topics. Yet, others are troubled by the perceived class, racial, and ethnic prejudices that shaped many of the moral reforms characteristic of the era. In turn, such conflicts may lead to ambiguity among progressive interpreters who approve of the political and economic reforms achieved by the movement but not of its moral flavor. Social disasters such as national prohibition create even more issues. Similarly, historians tend to focus on national issues and debates, although there is broad recognition that many of the progressive reforms were first debated and implemented at the state and local levels. In this hierarchy, the kinds of goals Marks worked for as a civic leader in Lamar, Missouri and Edmond, Oklahoma are not going to be given much serious attention and may not be considered progressive.

Marks' call for increased cooperation, education, and access to media clearly addressed means to augment limited resources and reduce the threat of parochialism to the advance of Christianity. His emphases were also consistent with others characteristic of the progressive era, and his three primary goals each directly mirrored parallel developments in secular society. Cooperation was the order of the day for business and helps explain the spread of fraternal lodges during the same period. Similarly, both political and religious reformers expected to improve their respective institutions by use of business practices. L. W.'s concern for education mirrored a broad national call for increased education at every level while his emphasis on newspapers reflected the phenomenal spread of print media and influence in the last half of the nineteenth century.[5]

Baptist progressives such as many of the faculty at Southern Seminary and other nationally known Baptist figures as well as ministers across the denomination also promoted a variety of programs to address the social problems of the era. Their push for orphanages, hospitals, poor relief, and similar measures differed little from those associated with the social gospel. The seminary was undoubtedly the most powerful voice for progressive values in the denomination and undoubtedly influenced Marks' beliefs. Although he never discussed that influence, the faculty and other speakers he admired and his personal reading during his time there support that conclusion. [6]

The seminary also encouraged a reconciliation of a social gospel with other Baptist concerns. Baptist social programs are often defined as social Christianity rather than social gospel because of crucial differences in emphases and methodologies. Personal salvation was always the starting point for progressive Southern Baptists and those who agreed with them. They shared the beliefs that Christians were called to address the evils of society and that the spread of Christian ideals and practices could lead to social transformation but only after individuals had been redeemed. Baptists would often support prohibition and Sabbath closing or assorted blue laws because they believed that society should be moral; they might even echo the spirit of a song of the prohibition era that "Every Day will be Sunday when the Town Goes Dry,"[7] but they expected their communities to be redeemed through the salvation of the people, not through institutional change or even moral reform.

These differences would magnify over time. The denominations responded variously to new methods in Bible study, the rise of fundamentalism, and the impact of the First World War. Even before those changes, however, Baptist progressives faced their own unique struggles within their churches and associations. Individual careers and sometimes institutions such as Southern Seminary were disrupted frequently by intra denominational disputes such as the Whitsitt controversy. Marks never faced the kinds of personal attacks many did, but his persistent calls to his congregations to abandon their narrower concept of the church helps to account for relatively short pastorates throughout his career. His career was also undoubtedly affected adversely by contemporary Baptist preferences for bombastic preaching characteristic of revivalism rather than the quiet, reasoned approach Marks preferred.

Such differences also help explain why he labored in vain to establish the Missouri-based *Word & Way* as the dominant Baptist paper in Oklahoma and the other disappointments he met during his career. He worked mightily to preserve Oklahoma Baptist College only to witness its sale on the auction block. Once *Word & Way* had failed, he contributed greatly to efforts to establish the *Baptist Messenger*. That newspaper would endure, but he would also have to witness a period of time in which it advocated stridently many of the causes and attitudes he had opposed. The ultimate blow to his hopes came when he finally realized he would not be able to obtain a pastorate that would offer him enough income to sustain his family, and he departed a full-time ministry.

The scope and nature of the disappointments he met could easily have broken him or caused him to abandon his commitments. But, Marks' was rarely completely discouraged. Oklahoma Baptist College had failed but Oklahoma Baptist University had gained an enduring foothold in the state. Despite the problems he may have had with the *Baptist Messenger,* it offered a unified voice for Oklahoma Baptists and frequently served the goals he advocated while the Children's Home would serve the needs of children for generations to come. More importantly, his progressive expectations were always secondary to much deeper beliefs. Devotion to God was the bedrock for his life, and his love for family both sustained and defined him.

He emphasized Baptist doctrine but valued the larger positive truths of the gospel message even more. He was committed to evangelism and the work of the church but to his family as well. He was an affectionate husband and loving, even doting father. He loved playing with his children in "big romps" and playing games, including dominoes, which were suspect among many Baptists. His love for young people did not stop at his family but included orphans and others he regularly brought to his home or generations of young people he led on camping trips to young people's retreats or church events. He relished hard work, frequently working sixteen hour days in varied activities from selling newspaper subscriptions or writing sermons to roofing a friend's house.

He held firm convictions and was always willing to confront any disagreement or practice that he saw as detrimental to the church. Yet, when he differed he always focused on teaching rather than exploiting differences. Likewise, he rarely allowed disagreements over church policy, denominational differences, or other issues to affect his relationships with people. When wronged, he reflected his agony in the privacy of his diaries rather than public forums. Even there, the harshest words he ever recorded about an individual were: "he does a lot of harm."[8]

At his most critical, he recognized the difference between his conclusions and the opinion of others, especially the judgment of God. For example, he regularly rated the sermons he heard, sometimes his own as well. On one occasion, he heard Sid Williams, a noted evangelist of the era. He was pained by the quality of the preaching he heard but then acknowledged that God seemed to use such preaching. That spirit of objectivity could also be seen in his rankings of the great orators of his day as well as those probably unknown outside a small section of a state.

His personal qualities and commitments offer a glimpse into the life and ministry of a remarkable, gifted, and loving man. His story adds to our understanding of

Baptist progressives of the era. It also offers insight into the life of small town pastors; the Whitsitt controversy; Lamar, Missouri and Edmond, Oklahoma politics; and, the growth of Baptist work in Oklahoma. He undoubtedly did not accomplish all he set out to do, but he remained active in associational and denominational work until his last years, was a respected member-teacher in his home church until the very day of his death and remained faithful to his commitment and his calling. In short, he modeled the kind of Baptist he wanted to lead others to become: he was not a lop-sided Baptist.

1. L.W. Marks, " The Power of a Creed, " unpublished research paper, ca. 1898, in Marks' miscellaneous writings,: "The Story of Oklahoma Baptists," unpublished manuscript, Marks historical writings, 154, the L. W. Marks Collection, the Oklahoma Baptist Archives, 154 (hereinafter cited as Marks Collection).

2. J. M. Gaskin, *Building A Denomination* (Messenger Press, 1992) 27.

3. Excellent discussions of historical treatments of Southern Baptist progressives are found in: Paul Harvey, "Southern Baptists and the Social Gospel," *Fides et Historia*, XXVII, #2, 59-77;and Keith Harper, *The Quality of Mercy, Southern Baptists and Social Christianity, 1890-1920* (The University of Alabama Press, 1996) passim and especially 1-34 and 113-119.

4. Stephen Fife-Adams, "Historiography: The Progressive Era," 1-2 <www.helium.com/ton/105073/historiography-american-progressivism-notable>.

5. Harper 30-31, Harvey 62-64; and, John W. Storey, *Texas Baptist Leadership and Social Christianity* (Texas A & M Press,, 1986)57-59, 68-73 and 124

6. Harper 30-31, Harvey 62-64; and, John W. Storey, *Texas Baptist Leadership and Social Christianity* (Texas A & M Press,, 1986)57-59, 68-73 and 124

7. Jerome-Mahoney recorded by Edward Meeker, Edison recording, ca. 1918.; see also: *Advancing Progressive Orthodoxy: William Owen Carver and the Reconciliation of Progress and Southern Baptist Tradition*, Auburn University doctoral dissertation,, 2005 as reported at <http://etd.auburn.edu/etd/handle/10415/653>.

8. L. W. Marks diaries in Marks Collection (hereinafter cited as Marks' diaries), Nov. 27, 1902.

CHAPTER 1

The Family, The Faith, The Man

Luther Whitfield (L. W.) Marks was born near the village of Benjamin in Lewis County Missouri on February 1, 1862. The fifth child of George Edward Cecil and Mary Jane Marks, he and his siblings and assorted cousins represented the fifth generation of a family whose migrations on America's frontiers mirrored the history of the nation at the time. Related values and the impact of hardships spawned by the Civil War shaped his character in many ways. More important to his story, he was born into a loving, extended family noted for strong Christian commitments.

That part of the family tradition may have had roots as far back as the Reformation, but it may be traced definitely to L. W.'s great-grandfather, John Marks. He was converted at the Montgomery Baptist Church in Montgomery County Pennsylvania and was baptized four months after the church had hosted one of the most important preachers of that day. In April 1740, George Whitefield, one of the leading preachers of the Great Awakening, visited the Montgomery Church.[1] Although Whitefield was a Methodist, his appeal and influence crossed denominational lines, and his "new light" preaching transformed the practices of existing churches, including Baptists. His fame as an orator had drawn even Benjamin Franklin to hear him, but his greatest influence was in shaping a renewed commitment to broad evangelistic appeals. His influence on the Marks family possibly explains L. W.'s middle name as well as John Marks' conversion.[2]Twenty-one years after his conversion, John Marks joined with others from the Montgomery church to carry the new light emphases to the newly organized Loudon County Virginia where Separate Baptists had launched widespread evangelizing efforts in that colony seven years earlier. Marks began preaching at the Ketoctin Baptist Church which hosted the first meeting of Baptists in the colony in 1765. That meeting led to the formation of an association which took its name from the Ketoctin church. Although John Marks was described as a "dry and phlegmatic preacher," he served as a model of Christian consistency throughout his life and successfully passed his faith, though not his denomination, to his descendants.[3]

His grandson George S. Marks followed his grandfather's model by moving to new frontiers and helping to establish a church there. He moved from Virginia to Illinois before finally settling in Lewis County Missouri in 1839. Locating in Lewis County six years after its organization, George quickly established himself as a prosperous middle class farmer and a leader in the Centenary Methodist Episcopal Church. Besides building their farms and churches, he and his neighbors joined in making the northeast corner of Missouri that state's "little Dixie."[4]

In 1849, his son George Edward Cecil Marks, a young man of nineteen, left Missouri to join another American migration, this time to the gold fields in California. He probably journeyed with A. K. Henton who died in California the following year. Marks returned to Lewis County within a few years and took up farming, possibly supplementing his income as a tanner. In 1854, he married

Mary Jane Henton, A. K. Henton's daughter and the descendant of migrants from Kentucky who were also noted for their strong Christian commitments, as were the newlyweds. George maintained a personal log that included references to his bible studies and Mary Jane studied her bible daily.[5]

The new family soon seemed on the road to a stable and happy life, but that prospect faded quickly. Three sons were born in the next four years, but two died within months of their birth. A daughter, Catherine, joined the family in 1860. Then, George Marks was killed shortly after L. W.'s birth. According to family traditions, George Marks missed L. W.'s birth because he was serving as a captain in the army of the Confederacy. There are, however, no records of his enlistment, other service, or reports of his death. That means that he was possibly part of one of the irregular units that Union supporters referred to as bushwhackers. A cousin William A. Marks was part of such a unit when he was killed by Union troops in April 1862. Although there are no records preserved from his enlistment, it is also possible he joined with a number of his cousins from the Marks and Cunard families who had elected to enlist in a unit of the Missouri State Guard which was formed in July 1861 under Colonel M. E. Green and that some how his enlistment was lost. The family members' enlistment coincided with one of the first battles to be fought in Missouri and directly threatened the immediate area of Lewis County. On July 21, Union forces under Colonel David Moore launched a campaign against secessionist forces in northeast Missouri with an attack at Etna in Scotland County before concentrating his forces at nearby Athens.[6]

In the midst of the resultant chaos, George Marks took leave from military duties to visit his infant son and others in his family. At some point in his journey, he was killed by Union forces near Florida, Missouri on July 22. This left his widow and three small children on the verge of impoverishment in the middle of a war that threatened their very existence. The details of her struggles or of other events in the family's history during most of the next twenty-five years have not been preserved, but the family was never threatened physically. A Union victory at the battle of Kirksville in August 1862 effectively ended significant military campaigns in northeast Missouri. That victory also insured the region was largely safe from the terrors of guerilla warfare. In this environment, there were even instances when the frontier spirit of neighborliness transcended the division caused by the issues of the war. For instance, a group of thirty loyal Scotland, Knox, and Clay County citizens signed a petition on behalf of a new pastor who had been accused of guerilla activities.[7]

Nevertheless, the Marks family status was precarious at best. George Marks' secessionist activities put the family at risk of legal actions adding to the financial pressures that threatened Mary Jane's hold on her property even after the war. There was a marked rise in lawsuits against guerilla neighbors in 1866, but that year marked the peak of postwar tensions, though some legal issues remained for decades.

These facts probably explain why the probate of George Marks' estate was not completed until 1877. The family managed to hold onto its land during the war and in the period of political and economic reconstruction which followed, but this proved small comfort. George Marks' estate barely covered his debts. Most of the money others owed him had been pledged in Confederate money or was owed by those impoverished by the war.[8] Although he had owned about 100 acres, associated debts and probate costs ultimately left his widow with credits for less than $500.00 when the probate process ended and her land was finally sold. Most of that amount had already been advanced to her by her father-in-law George S. Marks, the first administrator of the estate.

The family's plight was compounded by post war economic conditions. Lewis County, as other agricultural regions in the state, took years to recover from the war. An economic boom south of Lewis County along the line of the St. Louis and Hannibal Railroad partly offset this pattern, but declining agricultural prices, high interest rates, and other problems threatened the livelihood of farm families in general throughout Missouri and the nation.[9] These developments meant that Mary Jane and her children were both impoverished and dependent on extended families facing their own resource pressures. Her woes were compounded by the accidental death of her oldest son in 1871, leaving only L. W. and his sister Catherine. Faith and family sustained mother and children during these difficult years. L. W. later memorialized his mother as the finest Christian he had ever known.[10]

Mary Jane Marks' efforts were supplemented by Marks and Henton relatives alike. Her father-in-law, George S. Marks, gave the primary support and helped the struggling family, advancing her money from her husband's estate and then from his own. By the time of his death, he had subsidized the family to the point that he felt it necessary to reduce her legacy and that of L. W. and Catherine in order to preserve any semblance of a fair share to his other descendants. One of Mary Jane's relatives, either her uncle or brother—both named W. D. Henton—served as trustee of George E. Marks' estate and also assisted the family in varied ways. Her brother would later encourage L. W.'s early ministry serving on the board that gave the young minister his first full-time employment in Christian service.[11]

A strong pattern of family support touched all aspects of L. W.'s life and persisted into his adult years. Someone in the family could always be counted on to provide financial help as well as other encouragement for his education and ministry. An uncle, Mat Marks, encouraged L. W.'s early spiritual development and later assisted him in his ministry. His sister and her husband did likewise; while an aunt, Miranda Henton Mitchell, offered similar support through much of his adult life. Known as "Aunt Ran," she lived to be the favorite aunt of his children.

Thus, whether he studied his ancestry or his immediate family, the young Marks found strong foundations for his own commitments. The spiritual support provided by the Marks and Henton families also contributed to other qualities. The family legacy included a gentle, loving spirit that would later be measured in his toleration and empathy for people. Family bonds were communicated in many ways including nicknames for most. While a child, L. W. became "Whittie" to family and friends. He later abbreviated his name to "Whit," but he used his initials for his professional identification.

Marks' family traits balanced a rigorous framework of faith permitting him the freedom to grow as a person and in his own relationship to God. A measure of that freedom can be seen in one of his youthful prayers that subsequently became a part of family lore: "We thank you, Lord, for what we've got; we hope there's more back in the pot." [12] Yet, for some reason, he delayed a public declaration of his faith until 1885 and then joined a Baptist Church.

The delay was consistent with family tradition and his circumstances. Despite the cultural expectations of his era which seemed to expect dramatic conversions, often a visible rejection of paths of conspicuous un-Christian lives, Marks evidently maintained a devoted life throughout his youth. Moreover, he never fully embraced the evangelistic expectation, emphasizing instead the commitment to belief and corresponding action. A related focus on doctrinal issues explains his decision to become a Baptist.

His disagreement with an overemphasis on emotional conversions typical of revival culture would be seen in a sermon he would later preach based on Acts 4:42, asserting that the continuance of practice was the only true test for conversion. Another message focusing on the importance of doctrine stressed these points in a different way. He began with the assertion that truth or falsity was the first concern of doctrine because it was the basis by which the mind must be convinced. In turn, the mind may influence the will. God promotes convictions through scripture and the work of the Spirit. That interaction then influences the emotions in a positive way in contrast to the tactics of some evangelists "who are all too often like fishermen who really land nothing."[13]

L. W.'s personal decision probably followed extensive study and took place in conjunction with changing family circumstances and general dissatisfaction with his prospects as an adult. He had assumed responsibility for support of his mother by 1880, working as a farm laborer and in a small store. He was devoted to his family, but he hoped for broader opportunities than those he could find in the confines of Lewis County.

He made his profession of faith in response to the preaching of Dr. D. T. Morrill who was holding a revival meeting at the New Providence Baptist Church near L. W.'s home in the Benjamin community. [14] It was not unusual for rural church people to attend services of other denominations, and some churches in Lewis County even alternated between Baptist and Methodist preachers, pleased to hear anyone who might be available. Neither the content of Morrill's sermon nor L. W.'s thoughts about his decision were preserved, but he probably chose to become a Baptist in response to a presentation of doctrines about the church. For Baptists, these meant an emphasis on autonomy of the local congregation, the absence of hierarchies, democratic organization, and similar principles historically associated with the denomination. Both Marks' mind set and his practice as a minister affirm the importance he gave to doctrine. Likewise, his subsequent preaching and counseling efforts focused on systematic presentations of the claims of the gospel. However, he never let those emphases dominate what he called the "positive truths."

At their simplest, these were the historic Christian teachings summarized in the Apostle Paul's stress on "Christ and him crucified." In Marks' view, this teaching mandated a focus on God's love, the person of Jesus, and correct views of sin. The resultant message offered both the hope of salvation and the promise of changed lives. For Marks and other progressive clergymen, the redemptive powers of the blood of Christ led to transforming the life of society as well as for individuals even as it strengthened the appeal of Christianity. In response, a great advance powered by the ideas and techniques of the modern world coupled with the historic truths of Christianity would follow.

Three sermons he preached at some point in his ministry illustrate his commitment to doctrine. In a sermon based on II Peter 1:16, he focused on the idea that Christianity rests upon a groundwork of fact rather than "cunningly devised fables." These facts included those found in the life and example of Jesus, the testing of his precepts and the transformed lives of his followers. For L. W., the affirmation of truth protected believers from heresy while strengthening their witness to the world. Marks addressed his primary reasons for his Baptist commitment in an undated sermon entitled "Why I am a Baptist Defined." He acknowledged that Baptists held a body of truth in common with many others, but they were also committed to "sound fundamentals" not held by others. These included the use of the Bible as the only rule of faith and practice, a converted church membership, congregational government, believer's baptism, and restricting communion to believers. Significantly, he focused more on the issue of the timing of baptism than on its mode. Even more noteworthy in terms of long-term Baptist concerns about the issue, his notes do not call for restricting communion to the members within a local congregation, as advocated by those calling for "closed " communion. A third sermon addressed soul competency, a focus on individuals vs. groups, and the doctrines that Jesus was the only mediator between God and man. While arguing for these doctrines, Marks also noted their practice could make churches either better or worse. At best, a congregation would function in relative harmony as individual members sought God's will and practiced brotherly love. At worst, they could foster a climate wherein a congregation would be torn apart by rampant individualism. [15]

Such distinctions defined Marks' commitment, but their appeal among Baptists in an isolated village such as Benjamin, Missouri might appear improbable at first glance. Many rural areas and small towns remained provincial island communities, where new ideas were treated as suspect if not inherently dangerous. This tendency was often reinforced within the churches, and Baptists as a whole were among the more particularistic denominations of that era. Southern churches were even less sympathetic to progressive ideas. Yet, the marriage of the Great Awakening and rural culture had also created counter forces that complemented the character that Marks had acquired from his family and possibly from preachers he heard.[16]

There was a generalized appreciation for shared religious experience, and neighborliness was portrayed as akin to godliness. Preaching often focused on differences and even included regular attacks on other denominations, but members from the competing groups regularly attended the revivals or social events of other congregations and afforded hospitality to all ministers. In effect, these practices produced an early form of the kinds of cooperation envisioned by progressivism and later by ecumenicalism.

In turn, the revivalist culture of the era also contributed to the progressive hope. Churches expected and often witnessed dramatic conversions. "Getting saved" was an emotional experience that could produce "shouting" or other forms of ecstatic—and noisy—celebration. Virtually every evangelist told stories of drunkards and other conspicuous sinners who had been transformed by the "power in the blood." Likewise, most communities knew of parallel instances within their own circle. Such expectations often led to excesses and abuses and even resulted in some people delaying conversion as they awaited some momentous experience. Yet, the promise of redemption and the reality of changed, individual lives also strengthened the progressive vision; if individuals could be transformed, then communities and nations might as well.

Baptists also had institutionalized a number of practices that lent themselves to Marks' progressive ideals. By the time of his conversion, Baptists had been linking together in associations for more than 250 years. These associations were based on voluntary agreements among local churches with shared beliefs and practices. From their English beginnings in the mid-seventeenth century, these historic alliances served two primary functions. First, they provided a means for cooperative actions among churches that were otherwise totally independent and frequently jealous of that status. Second, associations provided opportunities for exchanges among people who were otherwise isolated. The first instances of such cooperation included the issuance of statements of faith or covenants which offered the basis for some standardization of Baptist doctrine. Later, the associations sponsored other cooperative endeavors ranging from the creation and support of missions or maintaining higher education efforts to the distribution of evangelist tracts.

The earliest associations frequently functioned in advisory capacities to local churches on questions of practice and doctrine. Associations added responsibilities for missionary and other purposes in the American colonies as the frontier and the Great Awakening moved westward. The first association in the American colonies formed at Philadelphia in 1707 . That organization fostered the growth of the Montgomery church where John Marks was converted. His subsequent role in the formation of the Ketoctin Association illustrates the continuing success of this model of cooperation.[17] By L. W.'s time, improvements in transportation permitted annual meetings at district, state, and national levels as well as the regular support of associational missionaries who worked among the churches and the unconverted within the associational boundaries.

In L. W.'s time, the Northern Baptist Convention was still organized as an umbrella organization for independent associations in the northern United States. In contrast, the Southern Baptist Convention was formed from the individual churches rather than the varied associations. State organizations in the South also tended to follow the convention format, but the state Baptist organization for Missouri was known as the Missouri Baptist General Association until well into the twentieth century.

Associational efforts in education and publication increased markedly in the decades following the Civil War. Statewide, Missouri Baptists were supporting fourteen different colleges in 1895. One of these was LaGrange College, where Marks would begin his post public school education. The Wyaconda Association, comprising churches in Clark, Knox, and Lewis Counties, the latter Marks' home county, had chartered the school in 1859 and supported it thereafter.[18]

As associations grew, many of their goals were promoted by newspapers dedicated to publicizing Baptist endeavors. Most of these journals were published independently, relying upon subscriptions, fees and the same advertisers as did secular papers to make a profit. Although most received no monetary support from associations or conventions, endorsement by such entities could mean the difference between survival and decline for a struggling newspaper.

Competing colleges and publications inevitably led to varying levels of animosity between different organizations within the Baptist fold. College rivalries were only the latest form of tension which regularly threatened associational harmony, especially in the South. Most of these threats arose from one of two related sources. The first was the provincial nature of the South which often led to a general suspicion of any outside individual or organization, thus threatening the very foundations of associational and other cooperative efforts among Baptists. The second conflict came with frequent debates over doctrine and related practice.

America's frontiers were fertile grounds for religious sectarianism. Many regions developed unique beliefs or traditions, often the product of a small group of preachers. These doctrines then often became linked to other aspects of regional identities. Southern Baptists were especially susceptible to these influences as they spread rapidly on frontiers and held to no formal creeds. The Landmark Movement, which was a principal source for many of the most divisive debates in the nineteenth century, illustrates this pattern. That name was given to a body of teachings most closely identified with J. B. Graves who edited the *Tennessee Baptist*, a state denominational paper, from 1848 until his death in 1893. Landmarkism endorsed six linked teachings that had implications for virtually every area of denominational practice. These were as follows: (1) Baptist churches were the only true churches in the world, (2) the true church is a local visible institution, (3) the churches are the only earthly manifestation of the Kingdom of God, (4) there must be no pulpit affiliation with non Baptists, (5) only the true church can administer ordinances such as Baptism, communion, and preaching, and (6) Baptist churches have existed since the time of Christ in unbroken succession.[19]

The tensions which arose from disputes over these and similar doctrinal issues were inseparable from other characteristics of the churches and people of the Southern Baptist Convention. The rapid growth of Baptists in the South had produced a diverse group. While united on many crucial doctrines, they were also deeply divided by socioeconomic standing, political beliefs and their degree of attention to Landmark teaching. The influences of urbanization and education were especially noticeable. Many of the convention's more prominent leaders came from the larger cities of the South. These individuals were much more likely to be better educated, open to progressivism, and less likely to hold all of the beliefs sacred among Landmark proponents.

On the other hand, rural Baptists often harbored deep suspicions about urban areas, depicting "city slickers" as both objects of scorn and suspicion. If they valued education, it was of a limited kind defined by the possibility for practical applications. Their definition might even acknowledge the potential contributions of higher learning but only so far as it seemed to offer a means of strengthening doctrinal or other proofs cherished by a particular group. These inherent tensions in the convention were exacerbated by other factors as well. The small town and rural forces often recognized that their ways of life and influence were in decline in the nation. The widespread impact of "lost cause" teachings, populism, and other provincial movements reinforced a pervasive fortress mentality and shaped every aspect of a Southern life still affected by the aftermath of the Civil War. Accordingly, much of the appeal of Landmark teachings was its claim to exclusive possession of the truth.[20]

By the time of Marks' conversion, Missouri Baptists were enjoying a period of relative calm, but the scars from prior political and doctrinal battles were still fresh; old enemies were in decline but still had the strength to oppose and divide. Prior to the Civil War, the state's Baptists had succeeded in organizing after decades of constant struggles against forces which opposed organized support of missionaries and evangelist outreach and a state wide association. Statewide support of William Jewell College was also an issue for the associations which were sponsoring their own colleges.

The Civil War and related issues then added new stresses to the hope for Missouri Baptist cooperation. Most Baptists opposed an ironclad oath in the state constitution of 1865, which required that elected officials, ministers, and other elected officials should be removed from their positions. A Wyaconda Association reported this would silence the majority of the thirty-two ministers who had staffed churches in the association before the war, and Baptists' traditional defense of the separation of church and state strengthened the opposition. However, some Baptist groups united to form a new Northern-oriented convention. State Baptists reunited in 1869 but could not agree on single alignment with either the Northern or Southern Baptist Conventions.

Landmark-related controversies exacerbated the division. State Baptists' meetings in 1873 and in 1876 had fought acrimonious battles over three related issues: financial management, William Jewel College, and endorsement of a newspaper for the association. Changes implemented in the next few years mollified most of those concerned about finances except those who remained suspicious of any central authority. The next two issues were not so easily resolved as they were both connected to Landmark issues and controversial personalities. The supporters of the varied associational-sponsored schools had long resented exclusive state support of William

Jewell College. In 1873, their concerns focused on Norman Fox, a faculty member at William Jewell College. [21]

Fox had graduated from Rochester Theological Seminary in 1857. He went on to serve as pastor of a Baptist congregation in Whitchall, New York and as chaplain to a New York regiment for two years during the Civil War. He became one of the editors of the *Baptist Record* newspaper based in St. Louis and then for the *Central Baptist* newspaper, the official newspaper for Missouri Baptists. He joined the faculty at William Jewell as professor of history and literature in 1868.

Within a few years, Fox's teaching brought him into conflict with Landmark forces when he challenged their belief in an unbroken succession of churches from the first century to contemporary Baptists. The resultant conflict nearly destroyed the *Central Baptist*, William Jewell College, and state denominational cooperation. In response to bitter attacks from state Baptist newspapers and convention debates, Fox took a year-long sabbatical to Europe before resigning his appointments in 1873. [22]

Fox's resignation and return to New York ended the firestorm, but shock waves from the controversy were still echoing decades later and far beyond the borders of Missouri. The efforts of David B. (D. B.) Ray alone would have assured that result. Ray was a Kentucky born Baptist preacher and newspaper man who moved to LaGrange, Missouri in 1873 to pastor the church there. By that time, he had already published two books, a text book on Campbellism in 1867 and *Baptist Succession* in 1870. . The latter offers some of the most detailed arguments for the unbroken succession of Baptist churches and is still in print in at least its 27th edition after periodic revisions. Ray had led some of the early attacks on Fox, and in 1875 while still at LaGrange, established the *Baptist Flag* newspaper. Despite his initial statement that the *Flag* was intended to occupy a field in polemic and historical theology rather than be a state paper, Ray sought endorsement by the General Association.[23]   H   e eventually obtained an endorsement from the association but never ceased his attacks on the work of that body and its leaders and even attempted to establish a rival convention at one point. He would continue publishing the *Flag* under a variety of names in Missouri and Oklahoma until its final designation as the *American Baptist Flag*.

Each of these battles had shaped Baptists in Missouri by the time of Marks' conversion. Some would play an even more prominent role in his own future, reinforcing his commitments and providing the foundations for much of his career and influence. He gained his education from Baptist colleges and the Southern Baptist Seminary; his first full-time employment was with an association, and he devoted much of his life to associational work even after he retired from a full-time ministry; and, his working relationships with Baptist newspapers led directly to his relocation to Oklahoma.[24]

Marks and Ray would meet frequently in subsequent years in Missouri and in Oklahoma usually representing competing newspapers. More importantly, they each represented two different visions for Baptist newspapers. One saw the media as a tool for polemics, the other to foster unity and understanding. Marks held little regard for Ray or his theology, but Ray, J.R. Graves and others would demonstrate repeatedly that newspapers could be used to promote narrower goals than those favored by progressives such as Marks. That fact shaped many of the subsequent battles among Baptists and frequently affected Marks' career.[25]

Marks and his progressive peers had little sympathy for those such as Ray and other Landmark proponents because they either impeded the creation and support of broad-based denominational structures or sought to use them for their own narrow purposes. Yet, most Baptists, including the most progressive, agreed with many of the Landmark ideas. They probably would not have been Baptists if they had not believed that Baptists were correct about their form of government and other doctrines and related practices. As a result, conflicts arose mostly over perceived threats to local autonomy from Convention actions and points, four and six, that called for avoiding pulpit affiliation with none Baptists and the assertion that Baptist churches had existed in unbroken succession from the time of Christ.

Landmark forces regularly fought against a wide range of cooperative measures from the establishment of state newspapers to the creation of a Sunday School board within the Southern Baptist Convention. The most extreme advocates were suspicious of any form of cooperation but most debates centered on charges that a proposed action actually threatened local autonomy. Marks invariably aligned with progressive arguments that the principle of local autonomy was not threatened by new methodologies or agencies; more important, he believed that these measures would facilitate the advancement of the kingdom of God.

Progressives largely ignored Landmark concerns about pulpit affiliation with those who were not Baptists and Southern seminaries routinely sponsored speakers from diverse denominational groups. The seminary's practices were criticized by Landmark proponents but did not usually lead to major debates although they undoubtedly reenforced the movement's suspicions of the seminary and individuals who participated in such exchanges were also suspect. Marks attended the seminary presentations regularly and sought out similar opportunities to hear preachers from across the denominational spectrum throughout his life.

Marks never defined his beliefs about the principle of unbroken succession though he was not likely to have regarded it as a test of fellowship between believers. That conclusion points to a significant difference between the leaders of the opposing camps. Marks and his progressive allies did not define themselves in terms of a polemic, seeking instead the means to rise above sectarian divisions to focus on what he called positive truths. That task was not an easy one, and it would not always lead to rewards commensurate with his efforts, but it was the one that would define Marks' ministry.

Despite the clamor from the *Flag* and similar sources, Missouri Baptists managed to establish a foundation for broad agreement under the leadership of Dr. Pope Yeaman. The capstone on his achievement came with the adoption of the "Missouri Plan" in 1889 which coordinated competing Northern and Southern mission programs under state Baptist administration. Even as the Missouri Plan was being implemented, Marks was beginning preparation for the ministry. He first entered LaGrange College, completing a college preparatory diploma in 1890. While there, he was given many opportunities to preach, obtaining his license in 1889. He was then ordained in his home church on August 16, 1890.[26]

Significantly, that event preceded another day of celebration in the Marks clan by only four days. On

August 20, his sister, Catherine, married John Higbie. The
newly formed Higbie family soon assumed responsibility
for Mary Jane Marks, providing her a home with them.
With the care of his mother assured, L. W. was now free
to focus on his education and ministry. His ordination
council included J. A. Minter and J. D. Hacker. The
former had evidently encouraged Marks' educational
pursuits and his decision to enter the ministry. Along with
L. W.'s uncle, W. D. Henton, Minter was a long time
board member of LaGrange College while serving as
pastor for churches in Lewis County and elsewhere during
his career.[21]

Completion of the course of study at LaGrange
prepared Marks for college work at William Jewell
College where he obtained a degree in 1895. While
completing that work, he also began his ministry serving a
number of small churches between 1891 and 1895. He
served as pastor at Shelbyville and the nearby Liberty
church during 1891-1893, as missionary to the Wyaconda
Association in 1893 and 1894, and then at Wheeling and
Meadville from 1894-1896. His time with the Wyaconda
Association was probably the only full-time job he held
during this period.

During this period, he usually served two or more
churches at the same time, a practice typical at the time.
The majority of Missouri's churches were small, rural
congregations, and only the largest supported full-time
pastors. Under this arrangement, a pastor might preach
one to three times monthly to a church. Often, this would
be accomplished during a single weekend when he might
preach on Saturday evening, Sunday morning, and
Sunday afternoon. Extensive rail connections—and the
traditional clergyman's discount for rail travel—
encouraged such arrangements.

Reports from these early years help to define the young minister, and there was strong continuity between his early commitments and those that would shape his later pastorates. For example, he was a strong promoter of missions in each of his churches and celebrated or mourned their responses to a variety of mission appeals. Significantly, one such appeal may have represented his first thoughts about Oklahoma, the foundation that would lead him to the emerging state almost a decade later. In 1895, the settlers who had claimed the Cherokee Outlet two years previously were on the verge of starvation following successive crop failures stemming from a regional drought. Churches, railroads, and other agencies of American life at that time cooperated in a massive effort to raise funds and ship food and other supplies to the starving homesteaders. The Baptist newspapers and churches of Missouri promoted the relief effort. The Meadville church, where L. W. was pastor at the time, contributed $8.00 to the fund. This was the only money sent in from that association, a significant amount at the time, and surely reflected L. W.'s advocacy as well as his personal contribution.[28]

Other reports from his early years of ministry reveal his typical devotion to work and general dissatisfaction with any level of personal achievement. L. W. worked both devotedly and systematically at any task he undertook. He worked twelve to fifteen hour days regularly and rarely complained about the demands of his schedule. He wrote of his work in the language of military campaigns and was never satisfied with anything less than total victory. Thus, in one year's service to the Wyaconda Association, he preached dozens of sermons, held five Sunday school promotions, made 289 personal calls, conducted four funerals, and held at least three protracted meetings, or revivals. At Alexandria, he worked with a congregation that had not had a pastor for two years. After two weeks, he left them with a pastor, some new members, including one conversion, and hope for their future.

He obtained his most spectacular results that year at Lewistown. He and the pastor there labored for two weeks, sharing preaching duties and often preaching to as many as three congregations daily. L. W. also led music and sang solos. The Lewistown revival produced twenty additions, nine by baptism. L. W.'s next "place of attack" was seven miles south of Labelle at the Salem school house. He canvassed the area and identified thirty Baptists within five to seven miles. He failed to get a church established but found "hearty support" that ultimately served as the foundation for a church. Still more meetings were held at the Lone Star school house, the Fox River church, Turner's school house, and Union. He ultimately preached in sixteen churches of the association. Net results for the year were twenty-two decisions by baptism, at least fifteen additions by transfer of letters, the foundation for one new church, and renewed vitality for at least three others. These were certainly acceptable achievements for the area and time, yet, L. W. felt the need to apologize to the Board. He comforted himself by acknowledging that "it is ours to plant and water, and God to give the increase . . ." but could not mask his discouragement.[29]

Collectively, these early ministerial experiences help to understand his subsequent pursuit of additional education and his growing devotion to associational work and promotion of Baptist publications. He saw both his own education and the spread of Baptist publications as tools to strengthen congregations. At the same time, his tendency to expect more from his own or cooperative efforts than could be achieved, even over a long period of time led to regular discouragement. He would leave positions following records of achievement others might have celebrated throughout his ministry.

His regular sense of disappointment also pointed to real problems of the churches at the time. The typical church was extremely small, often consisting of no more than two or three extended families. Twenty people might be considered a crowd, and wet roads, snow, or an illness in a family could mean no attendance at a particular service. Such churches could rarely support full-time preaching and were correspondingly dependent on local preachers. Often these men worked alongside their congregations during the week or in neighboring fields. These preachers were often dedicated men who compensated for a lack of formal training with intense study of the Bible and devotion to their congregations. On the other hand, many lacked necessary preparation. Others were inclined to a host of questionable interpretations that increased the Baptist tendency toward fragmentation.

Inadequate preaching was only the beginning of the problems faced by small, rural churches. The Sunday school movement was in its infancy and had not reached most of rural America. Even where it had, there was a scarcity of written materials for teaching or any other systematic presentation of the Bible. Likewise, many churches did not have music books, never mind organs or pianos to facilitate congregational singing.

The absence of full-time pastors often left churches under the leadership of a deacon or family head who often had their own agenda and opposed pastors who sought to lead the church. Many churches had traditions that required annual calling of pastors and routinely refused to support the call of any pastor for a second year, regardless of his qualities. And, woe to the preacher who challenged the pet doctrine of a family head or who mentioned the subject of financial accountability.

The vast majority of Baptist preachers could expect to be behind on their salaries throughout most of the year. Marks certainly faced such pressures throughout his ministry and in nearly every church he served. For example, he did not receive final payment for services at Meadville until three years after his departure from the church. Regular support of agencies, missions, or other efforts was even less certain, frequently leaving associational work and other vital ministries unfunded. Thus, the position he held with the Wyaconda Association was temporarily abandoned following his resignation due to funding difficulties.[30]

Small churches used three means to address these deficiencies. The first of these were annual meetings or revivals. These campaigns were used primarily as tools of evangelism with the typical church recording most, if not all, conversions for a year from revivals. Although most churches preferred to hold their annual meetings in the spring or fall, isolated congregations also held revivals in the hard winter months. In 1896, L. W. preached a revival at the Liberty church during December up to and including the week of Christmas. That timing was due to a limited supply of available preachers and also points to a second function of the revivals. They provided regular opportunities for rural churches to hear better trained, or at least different, preachers. Dr. Morrill's preaching at New Providence that produced L. W.'s conversion illustrates the importance of this practice.

Associations offered the second means to address the needs of local churches and to expose them to ideas beyond their narrow concerns. Annual associational meetings provided opportunities for ministers to study topics under the guidance of seminary faculty members or others, listen to the best preachers in a region, meet with and hear representatives from Sunday school or similar programs, and to fellowship with church leaders from across the denomination. Representatives from the different Baptist publications would also be present, publicizing their work and selling subscriptions.

In 1895, the *Central Baptist* was the leading Baptist newspaper in Missouri. The paper was established in 1868, merging two prior publications that had mirrored state Baptist divisions over the Civil War. The *Central Baptist* was privately owned but had become a semi-official arm of Missouri Baptists, despite competition from the *Flag*. The 1895 meeting of the Baptist General Association called the *Central Baptist* ". . . the acknowledged organ of the General Association of Missouri." However, the section of the association's report on the press also acknowledged the recent emergence of a "sprightly and vigorous Baptist weekly in Kansas City, called the *Word & Way*."[31]

Word & Way's aggressive marketing would later provide Marks' introduction to Baptist newspaper work as well as the incentive for his move to Oklahoma. In the meantime, he read it and the *Central Baptist* faithfully and other such publications when they were available. Likewise, he began attending district and state associational meetings regularly. He quickly assumed leadership positions within these organizations, serving on various committees and often as recording secretary. As early as 1895, he was taking some minutes for the Missouri Baptist General

Association which met that year in St. Joseph. At the same meeting, he met S. M. Brown, the principal figure in the growth of *Word & Way*.[32]

Typically, the notes of recording secretaries were the basis for reports in Baptist newspapers, so it is probable that Marks established working relationships with both the *Central Baptist* and *Word & Way* in conjunction with this activity. He published some miscellaneous reports in both newspapers during the same period. He also sold subscriptions for each, a practice many ministers used to augment their incomes.

Marks' first encouragement to attend the seminary likely arose from his educational successes or from associational or newspaper contacts. He enjoyed study and found academics relatively easy, although his spelling was inconsistent; he even misspelled his first daughter's name for a number of years. He was more concerned with practical applications of learning rather than ideas, but that concern provided motivation for his studies and added to his preaching and teaching.

The faculty at LaGrange or William Jewell may have recognized his gifts and urged him to attend a seminary. His interest may also have been stimulated by one of the ads or articles about seminary activities that were published regularly in Baptist newspapers and Marks' notes from the 1895 Missouri Baptist associational meeting in St. Joseph included references to a promotion for Southern Seminary where he would later attend. Before either of those events would take place, however, another factor began to shape L. W.'s ministry. On February 19, 1895, he married Sadie Jenkins with J. A. Minter performing the wedding. A Baptist girl from Scotland County Missouri, Sadie had visited relatives at Benjamin some time earlier where she and Marks had met. Sadie proved to be the helpmeet that complemented Marks' own dedication and faith. Thereafter, he regularly consulted with her on the varied crucial decisions affecting their family and his ministry. In each instance, he would report that they had prayed, reached agreement, and that she supported him fully.

During the next nineteen years, L. W. and Sadie became "Pop" and "Mom" to ten children: Zulah (1896), Paul Eaton (1897), Luther Whitfield, Jr. (1898), Mary Frances (1901), Wynona (1903), Walter F. (1905), Viola Joyce (1907), Marcus Marion (1909), Ferrell Cecil (1911), and Berta Lee (1914). The family's size would add to the financial pressures Marks faced throughout his life, but he found no greater source of joy. He did not, however, reflect such pleasure about the birth of his children in the diaries he maintained from 1898 to 1918. Subsequent generations of his family would read his diaries and muse that he seemed more excited about the birth of a new calf than a child.

There is a kind of truth to that judgment, but it misses two important points. First, a calf represented a potential source of income for the always financially strapped family. Second, L. W. shared the reticence of his time in speaking about such matters as the birth of children. The Victorian standards of the era precluded much discussion of such matters. Instead, the forthcoming birth of a child can be seen only in his references to changing household patterns or his increasing share of household duties. In contrast, when he was removed from his family for more than a few days, he always describes his longing for them, and his returns to them were followed by reports of a joyous homecoming often including time set aside for a "romp with the children."

As with his adherence to Victorian values, Marks was a product of his age in many other matters, but there were important exceptions to this pattern. He often seemed to take pains to assure his diary that he had offered "a firm second" to a visiting preacher's condemnation of dancing or card playing. On the other hand, he saw no harm in playing dominoes, also suspect among the devout, and regularly played at home despite Sadie's concerns about the practice. His playful nature also may have offended the sensibilities of those who expected ministers to maintain their dignity on all occasions. He liked playing with the children of the church as well as his own too much to adhere completely to that mandate.

In other respects, however, the people who knew him found little to criticize on other grounds. He was comfortable in any circumstances his work led him to. He seemed to enjoy sleeping on the ground or in the poor accommodations he often found in Missouri and Oklahoma homes. He probably equated such experiences with camping and the other outdoor activities he relished.

He balanced his playful nature with his devotion to work and firm convictions. He was almost tireless, whether working in ministry, in the fields, or other activities. His gardens would provide much of the food for his family, and he was a capable carpenter often working about the house, augmenting his income, or helping a neighbor with building projects. He valued work of all kinds, ranking it only after family and faith. And, his convictions required that he should be accountable for each day's activities. Often, he would conclude his entries with "a good day's work."[33]

His daily reports to his diary basically describe what he did plus references to occasional local and church events, the books he read, and similar topics, rarely giving attention to his feelings or thoughts except for three standard practices. He maintained a kind of spiritual goals inventory; reported on community or church-related discussions and conflicts; and rated many of the sermons he heard as well as those he preached himself. Marks often used the coming of the new year to define his basic goals. Typical entries included his hope to "become a better man" or his desire for a good "year's work for the Lord." At other times during the year, he would announce other objectives or evaluate his progress. These comments ranged from announcing his commitment to begin tithing to assessments of his or a congregation's responses to particular situations. At times of crisis, he often prayed with his wife, church members, or colleagues about varied concerns but was particularly prone to reflect on such matters in personal devotions. He prayed about every aspect of his life and especially his work efforts or what he hoped to accomplish.[34]

His reports on community and church matters include comments about his disputes or disappointments with individuals and groups. Broadly tolerant of human foibles and interpretive differences, he nevertheless confronted any disagreement or practice that he saw as detrimental to the work of the church, contrary to scripture, or harmful to others. This led him to support a wide range of community reform efforts but his commitment to church responsibilities remained paramount. This emphasis was consistent with his beliefs about the nature of Christianity and the church. He knew that both individuals and groups would not always do right or respond to the truth. On the other hand, he expected the body of believers represented in the local church to respond to the positive truths when they were presented effectively. Even when a church or individuals fell short of his expectations, he refused to permit it to affect his responses to people. He rarely showed any animosity toward his opponents, even when he feared their actions could disrupt the work of the church. He even agonized about seeking justice when he was wronged but never took actions to address personal offenses. In times of conflict, he usually decided that his inability to implement his ideas and programs stemmed from his own failures, never blaming others. When such disagreements persisted in a church, he would resign his pastorate.

He responded similarly in the larger communities where he lived. He accepted community leadership positions in varied roles and maintained positive relationships with most groups and individuals. He was open to ideas generally, respected a wide range of Protestant viewpoints, and regularly worshiped with Methodists and Presbyterians. He also attended services of the Churches of Christ, the Disciples of Christ, holiness groups, the Salvation Army, and others who shared a commitment to his idea of "positive truths."

He lamented Christianity ". . . rent asunder in an agony of conflict over a diphthong" or because of an ". . . overemphasis on some favorite truth." He advocated Baptist principles but only because he believed they were most correct. He was willing to debate when necessary and never retreated from his beliefs, but focused on teaching rather than exploiting differences. On occasion, he would renounce fellowship with a particular group but only if he felt they had betrayed clear scriptural standards. Even in such instances, he reflected on his decision in his diary rather than public forums.[35]

The one area where he revealed any evidence of a critical spirit was in his regular evaluations of sermons. His rankings ranged from "searching," "stirring," "moving," "forceful," and "practical," to "long and noisy," "noisy but not deep," "rambling," and "poor." Sometimes his evaluations described his impression of preachers rather than their messages. In one such instance, he referred to "a deadbeat Baptist preacher." On another occasion, he reported that a preacher had "cut some high capers." He wrote of another message as "a mess of sophisticated assertions. Made great impression. Women shouted tremendously."[36]

Although overtly critical, he also recognized the difference between his impressions and the actual value of particular sermons. He seemed almost at the point of agony assessing the poor quality of one noted evangelist's preaching but then puzzled about the Lord's use of such preaching. More often, his failure to rank a message he had heard might be as telling as some of his comments. He usually made no comment about evangelists, including those he worked with. Likewise, he rarely commented on the sermons of his own pastors.[37]

Otherwise, his criticisms did not seem to be affected by either a preacher's reputation or denomination or the length of a message. He responded favorably to "a magnificent one and one-half hour address." In contrast, he reported on a "very learned, very long, very dry sermon" by Dr. George C. Lorimer, a leading Baptist preacher of the day. On one occasion, he heard the noted Baptist orator Carter Helm Jones and pronounced his sermon as among the best he had ever heard. Later he heard Jones preach on "Blasting at the Rock of Ages" dismissing it with "not much in it for me."[38]

He gave comparable attention to his own efforts. He rated his better messages as "snorting good" or a "rouser"; at his absolute best, he would announce that he had "swept the deck clear." At other times, he would rate his sermons as "rather weak," "poor," "very poor," and even "I am ashamed of it." After one of his "fair" messages he went on to add, "Many of the folks went to sleep. I was nearly asleep myself."[39]

The latter comments, though not typical, suggest that Marks was not a great orator. Neither his personality nor his own convictions allowed him to use many of the preaching devices of his era. He consciously avoided bombast in favor of coherent messages that emphasized solid teaching. These characteristics would limit his appeal to many churches. His recognition of that reality together with his perceived failures in the first years of his ministry and his high regard for education explain his decision to enter Southern Baptist Theological Seminary in 1897. That resolution would be tested by extreme financial and family pressures the next three years.

---

1. "The Montgomery Baptist Church" excerpt from "The History of Montgomery County" as printed in anon, Krefeld Immigrants, Vol. 12 #1. 34-36; and Edward Matthews, History of Montgomery Baptist Church (Ambler, PA: A. K. Thomas, 1895) 12-19.

2. According to Freddie Marks who has conducted extensive research on Marks family genealogies, there is also the possibility the Whitfield name came from Catherine Whitfield that another source identified as a wife of George E. Marks, Freddie Marks to Alvin Turner, FAX, May 29, 1996; that explanation could also account for the selection of "Catherine" as the name for L. W.'s sister. However, Catherine Whitfield's name does not appear on the genealogies preserved in family Bibles. Additionally, L. W.'s middle name appears as "Whitefield" in his father's Bible.

3. Flora Davis Maull, Genealogical Notebook (Princeton, NJ: self-published, 1985) 81-87; Robert Boyle C. Howell, Early Baptists in Virginia (Philadelphia, PA: American Baptist Publication Society) from fiche #3081 0570, unpaged; Harrison Williams, Legends of Loudon (Richmond, VA: Garrett and Massie, 1938) 79; Charles P., Poland, Jr., From Frontier to Suburbia (Marcelina, MO, 1976) 44-48.

4. Extrapolation from family Bibles; unknown compiler, 1944, Marks family files; anonymous, *History of Lewis, Clark, Knox, and Scotland Counties, Missouri* (Astoria, IL: undated reprint by Stephens Publishing Co., original printing 1887) 794-796.

5. Copy of letter dated January 15, 1917, from W. M. Moore to Edward P. Cunard, regarding Stephen Cunard and Marks relatives; transcripts of varied obituaries and copy of George E. C. Marks personal log in Marks family files, the *Word & Way*, February 4, 1943: 16.

6. Moore to Cunard letter, January 15, 1917; Lewis County probate records, George E. Marks estate, November 9, 1962; Marks family files; Missouri Secretary of State Soldiers Data Base, August 27, 2009; The Missouri State Guard, "and Battle of Athens," September 24, 2007. 1-3 and 13, 1-3. *Wikipedia* ; and, Jeanne C. Eakin and Donald Hall, Branded AS Rebels (Lee's Summit, MO: Print America, 1995), <members.ad.com/ozrkreb/hist3msg.htm>. (December 2007).

7. Michael Fellman, *Inside War* (New York: Oxford U Press, 1989) 5-6, 10, 48, and passim; Gordon Kingsley, Jr., *Frontiers: The Story of the Missouri Baptist Convention* (Jefferson City, MO: Missouri Baptist History Commission, 1983) 57-63.

8. *Inside War*, 5-6, 10, 48, and 242-245; Marks' estate materials, Marks family files.

9. Ibid .

10. Marks' diaries, January 9-11, *1911.*

11. Lewis County Probate Records, George Marks' estate; George S. Marks' will, August 24, 1888, Marks family files.

12. L. W. Marks III interview with Alvin O. Turner, ca. August 1999.

13. Undated sermons based on I Peter 1:16 and John 7:17, Sermon files, Marks Collection.

14. Copies of related documents from Marks family files

15. Sermon files, Marks Collection.

16. Sermon files, Marks Collection, *Frontiers* 35-51 and 87-93.

17. H. Leon McBeth, *The Baptist Heritage* (Nashville, TN: Broadman Press, 1987) 211.

18. John P. Green, *The Growth of the Educational Idea Among Missouri Baptists* (Mississippi: Baptist Centennial, 1906) 7; *Frontiers*, 87-93.

19. Robert G. Torbet, *A History of the Baptists* (Valley Forge, PA: Judson Press, 1973) 18-20, 281 and 293; McBeth 456-553; W. W. Barnes, *The Southern Baptist Convention 1845-1953* (Nashville, TN: Broadman Press, 1953) 103-113; Robert A. Baker, "Factors Encouraging the Rise of Landmarkism," James E. Tull, "The Landmark Movement: An Historical and Theological Appraisal," and W. Margan Patterson, "The Influence of Landmarkism among Baptists," *Baptist History and Heritage*, X, Jan. 1975: 1-19 and 44-56.

20. The lost cause was a political and literary movement that attempted to reconcile continuing Southern claims of moral superiority with its defeat in the Civil War. A study of this movement is in *Baptized in Blood: The Religion of the Lost Cause* (University of Georgia Press, 1983).

21. *Frontiers* 64-65, 69-74; J. F. Kemper, "State Missions in Missouri During One Hundred Years," *Missouri Baptist Centennial, 1906*. 2. <baptisto_parchments.org/centennialbook>.

22. Ibid; D. B. Ray, *Baptist Succession* (Rosemead, California: The Kings Press, 1945) 51-56.; James G. Clark, *History of William Jewell College* (St. Louis, MO: Central Baptist Press, 1893) 223-224; George W. Lasker, *The Ministerial Directory of the Baptist Churches* (Oxford, Ohio: Ministers Printing Co., 1899) 268; W. Pope Yeamans, *A History of the Missouri Baptist General Association* (Columbia, Missouri: E. W. Stephens, 1899) 307-368.

23. *The Baptist Heritage* 59-60 and 749-755; excerpt from William Cathcart, ed. "D. B. Ray, D. D.," *The Baptist Encyclopedia*. <geocities.com/Baptist_documents/ray>.

24. E. L. Compere Inventory, Oklahoma Baptist Convention History, Box 10 #5, Southern Baptist History Library and Archives.

25. Marks' diaries, August 4, 1909; November 14, 1911; and March 3, 1914.

26. *Frontiers* 66-93, passim.

27. Copies of related documents in Marks family files; other materials include L.W. Marks' textbooks used at LaGrange College including D.B. Ray's book on Campbellism and J. R. Graves, *The Iron Wheel* .

28. Report, Linn County Baptist Association, September 21, 1894.

29. Reports, Wyaconda Baptist Association, 1892-1902, passim.

30. Marks' diaries, May 24 and Sept. 29, 1898.

31. *Frontiers* Kingsley 72 and 93-94; A History of the Missouri Baptist General Association 311- 313 and Marks' report from 1895 meeting of the Missouri Baptist General Association, Marks miscellaneous writings, Marks Collection.

32. *Central Baptist*, May 7, 1895.

33. Freddie Marks notes, Marks family files and Alvin O. Turner interview with Wynona Marks Holmes and Marcus Marion (Ship) Marks, February 3, 1996; Marks family files; for representative diary entries see: Marks' diaries, February 7 and 10, 1898; November 21, 1902; March 3, 1903; June 1, 1914; and June 1914, passim.

34. See for example: Marks' diaries, June 1, 1898 and January 1, 1902.

35 ."The Power of a Creed," Marks Collection.

36. Marks' diaries, March 5 and 29, 1898, August 19 and October 27, 1900, June 4 and July 19-21, 1905 and January 6, 1906.

37. Marks' diaries, April 6, 1898.

38. Marks' diaries, March 29 and May 31 1898 and September 12, 1909.

39. Marks' diaries, March 20 and April 20, 1898, October 27, 1900, November 19, 1905 and May 16 and 23 and June 4, 1908.

CHAPTER 2

Southern Seminary, Whitsitt & Disappointment

L. W. entered Southern Seminary at the comparatively old age of thirty-four seeking means to reach his goals. He was never interested in education for its own sake and was not impressed by degrees or other symbols of academic achievement. Marks always focused primarily on results, and he expected his studies to strengthen his ministry and his potential contributions toward the advancement of the church and its work. He could not have helped but hope that the seminary would also provide the means to enhance his career, but he had not left his wife and child primarily to prepare himself for bigger churches or higher positions. He was always happiest when with his family and would learn, if he did not already know, that his heart lay in small towns and rural America rather than the burgeoning cities of industrial America where the larger, more prosperous churches were located.

His beginnings at seminary and continuation were made possible by the unfailing support of his wife and extended family. John Higbie and others provided regular loans while the Jenkins family provided Sadie and his growing family a home during much of his time at Southern Seminary. His three years at the seminary would fulfill the vast majority of his hopes, complementing and affirming the directions, philosophy, and beliefs that he had gained from his family and in his first years in the ministry. Southern Seminary offered exactly what the young minister sought. It was one of the dominant forces in Baptist life at the time, shaping the denominational future with the faculty and graduates alike promoting the very values Marks cherished. These included support for a convention-wide search for efficiency and a corresponding call for organizational structures from Sunday schools to other boards to complement those goals for the denomination.

Despite stresses that arose within a pastorate there, frequent isolations from his family and the ever present financial struggles, his time at seminary also gave him abundant opportunities to grow as a person and minister. It also made him a first-hand observer of the culmination of the Whitsitt controversy.[1] William H. Whitsitt was president of the seminary from 1896 to 1898. He had earlier written historical studies about the beginning of the use of immersion among Baptists that directly challenged a key landmark assertion about the continuity of Baptist churches. A veritable firestorm of protests soon threatened the very existence of the seminary and even the Southern Baptist Convention itself. Marks' comments about that event and related concerns add those of a close and interested observer, suggesting it was much more complicated than a simple battle between progressives and reactionary forces in the Southern Baptist Convention.

On January 1, 1898, Marks entered the first entry to the diaries he would maintain through much of the next thirty years. He reported that he was "grateful to God for the blessings of the past year and favorable outlook for this one." His sense of well-being contradicted his immediate circumstances as he was ailing with a bad cold and headache. Instead, his successes the preceding semester in his first term at Southern; favorable responses to his first two months as pastor of the Jeffersonville, Indiana Baptist Church; and his sense of spiritual progress all supported his optimism about the new year. His stated goals for the year were to become a better man and to give special attention to the saving of souls.[2]

At the same time, he was hoping to find the funds necessary to bring his family to join him at Jeffersonville. The delay between his hopes and their fulfillment was the only problem he described in the next few weeks. On January 18, he reported that he had made "splendid papers" in the systematic theology class taught by Dr. W. H. Whitsitt. In the same entry, however, he acknowledged that he would "love to see my wife and babies tonight." The next week he received word from an uncle that the local bank had agreed to lend the money necessary to move his family near him. Rarely effusive, he wrote he was rejoicing at the prospect of seeing his wife and children.[3]

As the month drew to a close, he began preparations to spend two weeks in Missouri and made the arrangements to bring Sadie and the children to Jeffersonville. He finally arrived home on February 7, where he was especially delighted to find that his two-year-old daughter Zulah still knew him. He devoted considerable time in subsequent days to preaching in area churches and meeting with family and friends but also reserved time for "big romps" with Zulah. Once settled in Jeffersonville, he noted that he was "contented and happy with my little family."[4]

He had obtained a church in his first months at the seminary, and its proximity to the seminary indicates his standing there. The church was located at Jeffersonville, Indiana, just across the river from Louisville, and its 149 members made it relatively large by standards of that era.

A bridge near his home allowed Marks to walk to the seminary when a ferry was not available or if he was pressed for funds, as he often was. The church maintained a schedule of events that corresponded to its status as an urban congregation with regular access to a minister. They held services three times weekly on Sunday morning and evening and Wednesday evening, which Marks usually referred to as PMs. The church also offered Sunday school, a regular schedule of Bible study and prayer sessions on Wednesday evenings, and monthly business meetings. He had chosen to teach in the Sunday school, although this was not always expected of ministers at the time, and many churches kept the organization of the Sunday school strictly separated from the church. Marks usually conducted visitations on Sunday afternoons, Tuesdays following classes, and other occasions as required.

Although offering numerous advantages, the Jeffersonville church also presented him with many of the same problems that had frustrated his ministry in the past and would again in the future. There is some evidence of problems within the church before he came, and it was behind on his salary within months of his arrival. That problem persisted through his time with them, meaning he often struggled to meet educational and family expenses. Later his struggle with a church leader would add to his problems.

Assuming the pastorate in the fall of 1897, the church was already $3.00 short of its budget by January. That amount often represented a typical weekly collection from the congregation, so it was a significant amount at the time. The following July, he would note that only fifteen members had paid anything during his tenure there, and of those, only four had contributed regularly. He was paid in full the following week only to face new shortfalls in the following weeks. Marks responded to the issue in two different ways. He prayed that God would help him in his struggles against a desire for a better paying church, evidently believing he was where God wanted him to be. The next fall, he encouraged the creation of a committee on systematic beneficence to deal with the problem. That action produced the first resistance to his work as pastor, but congregational giving improved for a while.[5]

Besides his attention to financial matters, Marks also established programs and emphases characteristic of his role at all of his future pastorates. After months of encouragement, he was pleased to report the acquisition of new song books in the spring 1899. Significantly, the song books were those promoted in the pages of *Word & Way*. This emphasis also illustrates his commitment to modernization. He saw contemporary song books as a part of the overall commitment of the church to align itself with the principles of the modern age. He personally enjoyed singing conducted in the old way of "lining out" but remained convinced that such methods had been superseded by progress and the increased availability of relatively cheap song books.[6]

Marks also used music differently than in the churches of his youth, regarding music as an integrated part of worship. He often functioned as a music director, leading "quire" practices. Even when he did not lead, he sang in the choir as an example and to encourage the quality of singing he advocated. He regularly sang solos well into his forties and on occasion, might even sing for a shut-in member when visiting them.

Although the church's giving created regular problems for his own finances, Marks was most disturbed by what he perceived as congregational lapses in hospitality. In

August 1899, he reported that he had to provide housing and meals for a returned missionary after every family in the church had refused. The missionary then spoke at the church four days later, giving a "splendid" presentation, but no one invited him home. Marks was "mortified" and again offered the missionary the hospitality of his own small home. By the following November, he reported that he was out of patience with the people because they never invited guests of the church to their homes.[1]

In contrast to that issue, the church had managed to eliminate all of its debts and was beginning to consider investment in a parsonage, probably at his urging, by this time. He had also been encouraged by results of revival meetings the preceding spring, regular growth, and a joint Thanksgiving with the Methodist Episcopal Church that November. The sense of progress continued into the spring, but in reality the roots of major conflict had erupted in December 1898.

Early that month, he reported a conflict with an unidentified deacon that arose from what Marks believed was a misunderstanding, probably over the issue of giving. He reported that they had all prayed and cried together and felt a little better, but the seeds of problems had been sown and would grow quickly. By March 1899, Marks was again discouraged reporting that he was "so tired" and with "no prospect for rest here." The church had now fallen behind on collections again after showing some improvement in responses to hospitality needs. A systematic giving campaign in the fall produced the largest ever monthly collection the following month, but a series of conflicts developed in June that soon produced Marks' resignation.[8]

Early that month, Marks reported that a deacon had challenged his leadership and told him that the deacons were going to rule, and L. W. had to go. The next day, a number of church members heard of the conflict and expressed their indignation with the deacons and their corresponding intent to break up the ring that had controlled the church for so long. Marks devoted two different evenings to prayer seeking God's leadership but found no peace amid the conflict. He was particularly concerned about the announced intent of other leaders a few days later to oust the deacon from membership. His discomfort continued even as reports of possible financial irregularities emerged. Marks, an experienced carpenter, examined an area of the church where the deacon had reported supervision of, or personal replacement of, 1,200 shingles and acknowledged that it looked more as if 200 had been replaced.

A subsequent audit, however, was inconclusive, so the matter drug on, disrupting and dividing the church. On June 10, the church finally acted and requested that the deacon resign all offices. About half of the members in attendance had declined to vote, but Marks believed most of the members had been satisfied with the decision. Five days later, the deacon, who had refused to resign in accord with the vote of the church, told L. W. to resign and began overt efforts to align opposition. By the end of the month, one of the deacon's allies acknowledged to Marks that they were in the wrong but still urged him to leave.[9]

In early July, the opposition resigned all church offices in a business meeting attended by about fifty people. The remainder continued to support Marks, but he began to consider resignation. Contributions lagged sharply during the remainder of the month. Then, the opposition's announcement of their intent to withdraw from the church provided him the answer to a long period of prayer and frequent discussions with Sadie. On July 30, he shared with her his sense that he should resign if things did not improve, and she concurred.

After another extended season of prayer, he decided that it was God's will to resign. At the next meeting of the church, he announced his intention to leave after two more sundays in the pulpit. Then, a number of developments caused him to reevaluate his decision. Although discouraged by collections in early August, the church defeated the anti-Marks faction, electing two new deacons. Then, three additions to the church on the 20th and a groundswell of support, including pleas to stay from many, shook his resolve.

Nevertheless, he determined to stay with his original conviction and affirmed his intention the following Sunday. He then reported a sense of immediate relief and was even more pleased by his decision when the church then voted to pay him in full the amount that had accumulated through August. He did not, however, abandon his duties until later that week, baptizing three girls and maintaining his regular church visitation schedule while Sadie made final arrangements for sale of the household goods. They departed Jeffersonville for Missouri on Saturday with L. W. expressing the desire to take things easy, tan, and get "rusticated up" before returning to the seminary for his last year of study, a year he would have to spend apart from his family.[10]

While serving as pastor at Jeffersonville, L. W. was also active in associational work for the Salem Association of Indiana, as he had been in his home state, and wrote an article for *Word & Way* about the 1898 meeting of this association. Related activities included his work dealing with a "bogus preacher" who had earlier served the nearby Silver Creek Church. L. W. served on an associational committee to document this preacher's bad conduct, a charge of bigamy, and to prevent his reception by another Baptist church in the area.[11]

Associational commitments probably also account for his regular efforts on behalf of two black congregations in the area, although, he could have done this on his own initiative. In any case, he was involved extensively in helping one black congregation organize during most of the last half of 1898. He first met with the congregation in June to help them deal with a problem between the deacons and the pastor. He held follow-up meetings, sometimes as often as twice weekly, for much of the next month, counseling members and the pastor, teaching parliamentary procedure, and helping them develop other procedures for church governance. Later in September, he met with a group, apparently a split from the other congregation, and assisted them in preparing to organize a new church. That November, he preached at what was probably the organizational meeting for the new church.[12]

These actions were not as unusual as they might appear. L. W. was not immune to the racial assumptions characteristic of the age or his Southern heritage, and the 1890s were the heyday of rising American racism. Related assumptions and practices were as likely to be advocated by progressives as Southern populists. However, progressives such as Marks also made distinctions among classes of blacks that permitted them to work cooperatively with black churches. Ultimately, Marks' most important criterion for his actions was his recognition of the claims of the gospel. He would subsequently exchange pulpits with black pastors in Missouri, rate their sermons, and contribute to traveling black evangelists with the same degree of generosity and skepticism he directed toward their white counterparts.

His efforts on behalf of the association also led him to work with the nearby Silver Creek Church which apparently had fallen on hard times. L. W. was one of a number of area preachers who preached at the centennial for that church. He then wrote an account of the meeting for the Indianapolis *Baptist Outlook*. He also wrote other reports for *Word & Way*, *Western Recorder*, *Baptist Reflector*, and other newspapers during this time on topics such as tips for young men on the way to the seminary, ordinations, and other topics. The next year, L. W. arranged for his Jeffersonville church to host the annual associational meeting. Ironically, the meeting was held in his last week as pastor at Jeffersonville in August 1899. That meeting also ended his involvement with the Salem Association which he had served for at least two years as recording secretary.[13]

The two most important consequences of his resignation from the Jeffersonville church were financial and familial. The loss of the salary, even though it had been paid irregularly, meant that he would not be able to keep his family with him his last year at seminary. It also limited the funds he had available for tuition and his own living arrangements. He preached for various churches during a month in Missouri preceding the fall term, but income from those sources was inadequate to provide the cash cushion he needed.[14]

A loan from John Higbie, who also signed a note at a Missouri bank, provided him with some funds, but he was hard pressed financially through most of the last year at Southern. Even worse for L. W., he literally mourned for his family while absent from them. He wrote regularly to his wife, Aunt Ran, his mother, an uncle, other family members, and to friends in the ministry such as J. A. Minter. This kept him in contact with his loved ones but did little to resolve his sense of loss. Most weeks, his diary would contain at least one entry about his longing for his family.[15]

Marks never directly explained why he returned to the seminary the last year. Beyond family and financial pressures, he was concerned about his ability to meet his requirements in Greek but finally resolved they could "shoot him in the back if he failed." He also had to assess the potential impact of the growing convention-wide debate on the seminary president, W. H. Whitsitt. As early as May 5, 1898, that clamor had reached the point that Marks' longtime mentor, J. A. Minter, advised him not to take a diploma with Whitsitt's name on it. Marks decided to return only after a prolonged time of prayer and his resultant conviction that it was God's will for him to do so. He was also determined to finish what he had started and gain the education and experience the seminary offered.[16]

Marks' disciplined approach to study and his education from William Jewell were more than adequate foundations for the academic demands of the seminary. He studied consistently, frequently waking at four o'clock in the morning and working until 10:00 P.M. to concentrate on class work and the other tasks he faced as student, minister, and family man. He used his diaries to maintain his discipline often commenting after a day of study and other work that he had done a "good day's work." In a more playful mood, he might record that he "did my studies like a good boy," but in each case, he was holding himself accountable.[17]

As a result, he completed all course work with high marks except for languages. He rarely expressed concern about other course work, frequently noting that he had excelled on exams. In contrast, he struggled with both

Hebrew and Greek. He eventually became comfortable with Hebrew but never with Greek. Although successful in his studies, he reflected little real excitement about the academic or theoretical content of his classes. He was much more likely to comment on the satisfaction he gained from prayer or meditation in conjunction with his studies than with the content of his assignments or class discussion.

He showed little interest in ideas per se and rarely mentioned content or personalities from his classes. Two exceptions to that rule help to define his interests and commitments. L. W. always enjoyed humor so dutifully reported on an incident that took place in John R. Sampey's Hebrew class. When Sampey missed class two days before Christmas 1899, the students concluded that the good professor had forgotten his class and wrote "Christmas gift and departure of Hebrew children" (in Hebrew) on the chalk board before leaving.[18]

An earlier report on Dr. Franklin H. Kerfoot's discussion of traducian and alternative theories reflect another aspect of Marks' character as student and minister. While noting that the class and Kerfoot favored the traducian theory overwhelmingly, he did not bother stating his own view, though implying agreement with the rest of the class. His treatment of that topic contrasted sharply with strong and frequent affirmations of his standing on questions of personal doctrinal application such as the use of alcohol. For Marks, theories did not meet the test of practical doctrine or the standards of positive truths that demanded his response.[19]

Despite his apparent lack of excitement about ideas, he maintained a regular program of reading in addition to his studies. His reading included many of the classics and popular books of the era ranging from *Black Beauty* to

Little Dorrit and *The Merchant of Venice*. He rated books much as he did sermons, finding *Quo Vadis* "interesting but not very profitable." He gave his highest praise to Henry Drummond's *Natural Law*, J. R. Miller's *The Hidden Life*, and especially Charles Sheldon's *In His Steps*.[20]

Sheldon's fictional account of a Kansas town transformed by response to the question, "What would Jesus do?" has long been recognized as a seminal work in the progressive Christian vision. For Sheldon and many of his followers, the gospel required Christians to base every aspect of their lives on their faith. Correspondingly, the book has often been portrayed as a call for a social gospel, devoted to action for the amelioration of social conditions affecting the poor and others. Marks, as other Baptist progressives, was more likely to emphasize conversion as the foundation for social change than Sheldon but he responded directly and personally to the book

He would return to *In His Steps* at other times in his life but read it first during three days in August 1898. He commented on its impact daily and concluded that it had done him "lots of good." He expanded on that observation, reporting a sense of the presence of the Holy Spirit that made the year's struggle worthwhile. The day he completed the book, he resolved to begin tithing, placing fifty-eight cents, ten percent of his total cash resources, in a jar he set aside for that purpose. That gesture was especially noteworthy as he had been seeking work at a nearby shipyard the month before because he was so hard pressed for money.[21]

Although he read a variety of fictional and other materials, the bulk of his reading outside of class assignments was devoted to Bible study and a variety of Baptist newspapers. He maintained subscriptions to *Central Baptist News* and *Word & Way*. He also either subscribed to or borrowed copies of varied state-based Baptist newspapers. The *Western Recorder* was provided to all of the students, and other newspapers may have been also.

Beyond his study and general reading, he relished the opportunities to hear the wide variety of preachers offered by the seminary and churches in surrounding communities. The seminary regularly hosted speakers from across the Baptist spectrum as well as representatives from other Christian groups. Famed preachers, spokesmen for the Sunday School Board, the Salvation Army, and others all spoke at the seminary on a regular basis. Marks attended at least one such event monthly, and he also sought out opportunities to hear area preachers, seminary faculty and students, and evangelists who conducted meetings in the area.

L. W.'s age and maturity in the faith were seen in his relationship to his fellow students as well as in his studies and activities. The students followed the customary form of address used by faculty and by churches at the time, referring to one another as "Brother." Marks followed that convention consistently but was just as likely to describe his work with one of "the boys." The fatherly connotation of that terminology was reflected in his function as a mentor to many of the younger seminarians. He routinely reported on his assistance to one of the boys with their studies, finding preaching opportunities, or in completing the paperwork for their licenses or the courtesy passes provided by the railroad or for similar needs.

He even served as nurse for different individuals when they were ill. On one occasion, he visited New York Hall for the better part of a week, giving baths to an incapacitated brother. Marks' efforts in such ministries were possibly the most prominent among those from the students during his time at the seminary, but others shared his commitments. The seminarians' willingness to care for each other in such ways was particularly important because of their limited finances and the health problems characteristic of dormitory living at the time. Diseases could spread rapidly in such environments leading to serious threats to health and life; for example, two dormitory residents died in the spring, 1900.[22]

Earlier that school year, L. W. served as a student representative to a seminary board meeting regarding student concerns about the food offered in New York Hall. Besides his age and his approaching graduation, his selection may have been based on the experience many students had while dining at his home in prior years. He reported heartfelt agreement with the student concerns, depicting the food there as a personal "bug bear" that added greatly to the miseries he experienced apart from his wife and family.[23]

Many of the students as well as L.W. struggled regularly with finances. The seminary maintained a benevolence fund that gave limited subsidies to many students, all of whom were eligible for free board in New York Hall. Married students received some equivalent financial aid. There was also a loan fund which was supplemented by student-led efforts to generate sources of financial aid for their fellow seminarians. Marks headed the latter program during most of his time at Southern.

Nevertheless, most students relied heavily on borrowing or family support as seminary funds were always far less than the students could have used effectively. Despite such pressures, the students demonstrated a strong commitment to sharing and giving. They shared the limited funds they had with each other. They lent money if they had it and borrowed when they did not but also raised hundreds of dollars for missions campaigns and similar initiatives each year.

Marks' response to these pressures illustrates that pattern as well as his own commitments. The first year, he was so pressed for cash that he borrowed $5.00 from the student aid fund to purchase Christmas gifts for his family. Later that month, he received a loan from a Missouri bank. Upon receiving a pounding from the Jeffersonville church the same week, he proclaimed it a "red letter day." He then gave some of the food to a poorer family from the congregation. The next month, he lent $1.00 to a fellow student, hoping he would "not prove a rogue." The following year, after again borrowing money for gifts, he received a package of food from home. He shared that largesse with fifteen other brothers who had remained in Louisville during the holidays, pooling his food with theirs to enjoy a "feast."[24]

L. W. enjoyed his role as mentor, and the brothers responded by electing him chairman of the graduating class for 1900. He would later continue as an unofficial guide to many of the younger men as they embarked on their careers. In later years, he continued to intercede for those who sought positions in Missouri or Oklahoma and regularly wrote letters of recommendations for others and maintained correspondence with many, encouraging them as they faced struggles in their ministries or other aspects of their lives.[25]

The pattern of sharing and service Marks and his seminary brothers demonstrated in such activities directly reflected their Christian values. Marks' efforts also illustrate his lifelong emphasis on cooperation among believers, but he was never willing to push his own cause in the same way he would for others. He appreciated help when offered, but he held to a strong view of God's leadership in such matters. He drew upon the brothers at seminary and later as friends and fellow workers, cherishing them as colleagues rather than as connections. His relationships with the faculty were varied. He seemed neutral toward most, rarely mentioning any by name in his diary. The first exception to that rule was Franklin H. Kerfoot who gave L. W. books and wrote him when he was away from the seminary during the summer. [26] In contrast, Marks' diaries reveal underlying tensions with the seminary's president, Dr. W. H. Whitsitt, from his arrival until the latter's resignation to avoid the likelihood of the withdrawal of seminary support by the Southern Baptist Convention. Marks' responses to the conflict offer insight into the thinking of both seminary students and Baptist progressives to what has become known as the Whitsitt controversy.[27]

During the preceding thirty years, the leadership of Basil Manley, John A. Broadus, and others had earned a key role in denominational life for Southern Seminary. Those gains came with a bridging of deep denominational divisions that had produced a series of controversies and debates throughout the denomination's history about the seminary and other issues. There was, however, no certainty victory could be preserved; deep divisions remained within the convention, and seminary faculty and graduates regularly drew fire from Landmark polemicists and others. The seminary's regular hosting of speakers from outside Baptist circles implicitly rejected a key Landmark argument, and the programs advocated by the seminary produced yet other challenges. For instance, in 1891, Dr. Broadus had led the successful effort to create a Sunday School Board after at least four prior rejections of that Board by the convention.[28]

Most of these Baptist battles were focused on organizational questions rather than theology and were ultimately less threatening to denominational unity and progressive goals. In turn, the provincial characteristics of the membership meant that their most heated debates were often localized. Thus, Landmarkism often surged in one region or state while it lay dormant in others. Theoretical issues could usually be avoided because there was extensive agreement on more basic biblical teachings, and seminary faculty usually respected the denominational consensus. This meant confining theoretical speculation to the classrooms or journals most likely to be read by their peers. Their academic minds also permitted them some openness toward diverse ideas, including key elements of the Landmark principles which rested almost exclusively in interpretations of scripture. Even when controversial theories were taught, the discussions rarely extended past seminary boundaries. These tendencies usually insulated the faculty from the continuing suspicions directed at their erudition, but Landmark or other forces were primed to strike any time academic theories seemed to challenge key doctrines.

Given those parameters, historical methodologies and conclusions were the most likely sources of major conflicts because historians claimed factual evidence to support their argument. Thus, the application of the historical critical method to the study of scripture produced at least two disruptions among Southern Baptists prior to the Whitsitt controversy. The first was the case of Norman Fox at William Jewell College but it had few repercussions beyond Missouri despite the polemical work of D. B. Ray and others. In contrast, the Crawford Toy controversy during the 1870s had centered at

Southern Seminary and threatened its support within the convention, if not its very existence.

In 1856, Toy had been among the first graduates from the seminary. After a brief stint teaching, he was appointed to initiate Baptist work in Japan. A shortfall in convention funding and the start of the Civil War prevented the beginning of that work. In the meantime, he planned to marry Lottie Moon, the famed missionary to China, but she broke off that engagement as she did another to him in 1877. His doctrinal views may have influenced her second rejection of Toy.[29]

After time in the Confederate army and an extended stay in a prisoner of war camp, Toy resumed his education at the University of Berlin where he was introduced to German historical-critical methodologies. He began teaching at Southern following his graduation in 1869 as the first addition to the seminary's four original faculty members. He was accepted initially as completely orthodox, but his advocacy of historical-critical standards for proper historical interpretation eventually led to controversy. He maintained that scripture has two natures, the internal one based on the inspiration of the Holy Spirit and an external one consisting of the historical and other qualities that could be investigated. His corresponding advancement of arguments against the traditional understanding of the creation account in Genesis 1 and his acceptance of aspects of Charles Darwin's views of humankind increasingly separated him from the mainstream of Baptists while straining his relationships with his fellow faculty members. These matters came to a head in 1879 when Toy resigned under Convention-wide pressures and in accord with his personal desire to prevent further damage to the seminary's reputation and support basis. The firestorm averted, Toy went on to teach Hebrew at Harvard.[30]

In the meantime, Whitsitt had joined Southern's faculty as professor of church history in 1875. With Broadus' death in 1895, Whitsitt became the third president of Southern, and a new Baptist conflict soon began to simmer with the seminary at the center. The dispute stemmed from responses to articles Whitsitt had written previously for varied publications. These included four written for the *New York Independent* as part of a series of thirty-five articles that journal published on aspects of Baptist history. A better-known piece appeared in *Johnson's Universal Cyclopedia* in 1886, arguing that Baptists had acquired the practice of immersion from Anabaptists in 1641. That argument directly challenged the Landmark belief that Baptists retained an unbroken historical link to the practices of the New Testament church. Their responses to what Marks regularly called the "1641 theory" triggered convention wide debates and calls for Whitsitt's dismissal or the withdrawal of convention support from Southern. As the conflict spread, Whitsitt's defenses of his writing alienated many of his early supporters.[31]

Marks also reflected his personal concerns about Whitsitt in light of problems he was dealing with as a student and as mentor to the younger seminarians. Marks maintained files on "frauds in the ministry" throughout his time at the seminary. This effort may have been triggered by his work in the Silver Creek association, but it led to frequent correspondence with individuals on the activities of individuals charged with moral failures or doctrinal failings. One such letter included an unspecified complaint about Whitsitt. Another contained a complaint from a student and former Methodist minister named

Nigh who claimed that Whitsitt had misled him about opportunities for churches during his time at the seminary.[32]

Marks' diaries also offer a chronological account of the growing conflict and the evolution of his own thinking on the matter. In January 1898, Rev. Jonathan Rust of Nashville spoke at the seminary. His remarks were strongly in favor of Whitsitt. Students and others in the audience that evening responded variously with some hissing and others applauding. Later the next month, the *Texas Baptist Standard* printed an article by Dr. John T. Christian asserting that Whitsitt had written articles he had denied writing. For Marks, the "proofs were abundant and clear" that Whitsitt had lied about the matter. He expressed no judgment about what should be done at the time but Christian's article undoubtedly added to Marks' concern about Whitsitt's rectitude.[33]

Despite the growing controversy, most seminary business continued as usual. The embattled president continued to teach his classes and perform a variety of administrative duties. That April, he hosted a dinner whose three-hundred guests included prospective students as well as seminary students. Carter Helm Jones and other noted ministers spoke during the event. The dinner took place without overt references to Whitsitt's struggle, but the issue reached a climax the next month.[34]

On May 5, L. W. received a long letter from J. D. Minter advising him not to take a diploma with Whitsitt's name on it. The following day he received a copy of the *Western Recorder* containing an editorial by B. H. Carroll challenging Whitsitt's integrity, adding his support to John T. Christian's charges. Carroll was a widely respected leader among Texas Baptists and throughout the Southern Baptist Convention He had earlier depicted the arguments about the 1641 theory as a debate among academics but this time, he went on to argue that Whitsitt's historical theories were "the least point involved in this case." For Carroll, the main point now was Whitsitt's integrity and the unity of the convention which had been sacrificed to the conflict between Whitsitt and his opponents. For Carroll, this meant: "The Baptist heart has been wounded. Confidence is broken." Marks agreed that Whitsitt had been discredited beyond any hope of reestablishing his leadership. He went on to comment, "I don't see how any Baptist who read that article can defend Dr. W." The issue came to a head later that month when Carroll announced he intended to introduce a motion to the Southern Baptist Convention calling for the convention to withdraw support of the seminary. Now, even Whitsitt's friends and supporters joined to urge his resignation [35]

Significantly, Marks would retain a copy of Carroll's editorial among only a few other items from his years in the seminary. Together Minter's letter and Carroll's editorial had both confirmed Marks' prior concerns and added a new one, the unity of the convention. Minter's letter confirmed any doubts he might have had about the reality of that threat. For Marks along with many earlier Whitsitt supporters, the preservation of the convention had become the ultimate concern.

In the meantime, June graduation ceremonies approached. Despite Minter's advice, Marks had finally decided that he could not abandon the sacrifices and efforts that had been expended to reach his diploma. He accepted certificates in systematic theology, church history, polemics, and ecclesiology. Whitsitt spoke at the ceremony, but Marks made no references to the dispute. In early July, Marks was at a pastor's conference and heard that Whitsitt had resigned, effective in one year, rather than be the cause of the seminary's loss of funding. Marks reported gratification that Whitsitt had resigned early enough to avoid censure from the convention but lamented that his departure would not take effect sooner. Whitsitt's action apparently satisfied Carroll though as his son B. H. Carroll was in classes with Marks the next year. [36]

Despite such tensions, the seminary reflected little in the way of new tensions during the remainder of 1898. As the date for Whitsitt's departure neared, however, tensions increased. On May 12, 1899, the Board accepted Whitsitt's resignation by a large majority. The faculty, however, was less agreeable voting 22-20 to accept the resignation. At the same time, Marks reported "considerable soreness" among Whitsitt's supporters though not much had been said. L. W. opined that was because not much could be said, and he rejoiced the following day as Dr. J. P. Greene was appointed as interim president. [37]

Though no longer president, Whitsitt remained at the seminary through the end of the fiscal year. At a seminar in June, he gave what Marks called "a strong paper" on universal church theory as Baptist doctrine. His speaking apparently produced a minor demonstration by some of his remaining supporters, but the controversy was largely over for students at the seminary. Ultimately, as had occurred with both Fox and Toy, the twin issues of denominational unity and the preservation of convention programs increased the pressure on Whitsitt to the point that he resigned, effectively ending the threat to the seminary and convention. For Marks, however, questions about the 1641 theory remained until later that year. In October, he heard and an address by George C. Lorimar whose criticisms of the theory ended any doubts Marks had retained about that question.[38]

Marks clearly did not want to return to Southern for his third year at the seminary because he dreaded the time away from his family. He had fattened up, enjoying days of labor on the Higbie farm interspersed with area preaching opportunities. His reluctance was compounded by the response of Zulah who took "his departure bad." To stay, however, would mean to abandon the varied goals that had motivated his original decision to attend; his commitments account for his return in the fall of 1899.[39]

Upon returning to the seminary, he gave little attention to his classes in his diary other than occasional references to his struggles with Greek or class successes, focusing instead on his longing for family and financial woes. The exception to that were his remarks about a new spirit at the seminary and his admiration for the conciliatory leadership of E. Y. Mullens. In fact, Mullens' leadership qualities would do much to restore relative calm in the Southern Baptist Convention and foster the growth of the seminary and its preeminence in Baptist life. [40]

As L.W. no longer held a pastorate, this gave him increased time for singing lessons and even tennis. Beyond his activities as student leader and continued work on the frauds in ministry effort, he gave increased attention to pursuit of ministry opportunities and took every offer of a chance to supply vacant pulpits. Some of his interest was clearly motivated by financial struggles, as the occasional chance to fill a pulpit could provide much needed cash. A new loan co-signed by Higbie relieved some of his financial pressures his final semester. He also wanted "to do something for the Lord" so worked with a gospel wagon and taught Bible classes at both Walnut Avenue and 3rd Street churches.

February 1900 marked a turning point in his thoughts. A week after noting his fifth anniversary and describing Sadie as the "sweetest best wife" ever, he reported a clean sweep for a set of exams. He then began to focus on final stages of his studies and on employment opportunities. One particular success he gained at this time was being named the chairman of his graduating class but he had yet to receive an offer for a suitable pastorate when received his diploma at the end of May. [41]

Friends from Missouri, the seminary, and elsewhere recommended him, but to no avail. One church rejected him because he opposed their focus on Landmark teachings, but he offered no explanations for his rejection at others. He returned to Missouri at the end of May where the pattern persisted. After three months farm work, spending time with family and regular supply preaching through northeastern Missouri, he had gained only one glimmer of hope. He expected a response from Hannibal, but that prospect soon faded. At the beginning of September, he resumed his prior job with the Wyaconda Association. The association agreed to pay him $60 monthly but only on a temporary basis. Even that fell short of the $750 annual income he had earlier set as his minimum.[42]

By this time, Marks must have recognized that he faced a real dilemma. At a time when the majority of Southern Baptist ministers surveyed reported they had no education beyond common schools, one might have thought a seminary education would have sharply increased the demand for his services. In fact, the opposite was true, and that can be explained a number of ways. First, the overwhelming majority of Southern Baptist churches simply did not have the resources to afford a seminary-trained minister. The churches Marks had served prior to the seminary and in the two years following routinely paid as little as $25.00 or less monthly, and payment was never assured. That did not compare favorably with wages earned by a lower-level manufacturing employee in the cities or a crossroads store clerk. Moreover, there remained tensions surrounding higher education among Baptists. The memory of the Whitsitt conflict and other localized issues plus the continued polemics of those such as D. B. Ray made the possession of higher education suspect among many congregations.

His age would have been a problem as well for he was approaching forty with only small-town church experiences. Third, Marks had a number of traits that made him less attractive to the more prosperous churches. He evidently did not possess the superior oratorical skills held by those such as Carter Helm Jones and B. H. Carroll, and his quiet presentations alienated yet other congregations. There is also a strong likelihood that he did not fit into middle class urban churches that could have paid higher salaries. He was noted throughout his life for his personal cleanliness and corresponding assets, but he remained a product of Benjamin, Missouri, a man who loved rural life. Much of who he was and what he wrote and preached illustrated that his heart remained in small towns of the kind where he would spend his ministry. The values of rural America were roundly proclaimed by most leaders of that era, but there was a difference between remembering a rural past and cherishing its present. Similarly, middle class valued labor but undoubtedly would not appreciate a pastor who would help a neighbor roof his privy or who dug the baptistery for his church, as Marks did during 1901 at Wyaconda. Together these factors meant he would never gain a measure of prosperity or even financial security. It would also mean he would be representing progressive values among groups among the least prepared to accept them.

Two undated sermons illustrate the combination of qualities and convictions that he brought to his ministry. The first entitled "The Pastor" was based on I Timothy 3:1-7, II Timothy 2:2, and I Samuel 21:8. He asserted first the pastor was to be a good man, without reproach, standing in proper relation to his family and community. He also had to be careful that he did not allow small weaknesses to offset his contribution. He could be neither a priest nor a "society pet." The message stressed education, arguing that the day of the uneducated preacher was past. At the same time, he asserted that training did not always produce immediate gains and should not be sought for prestige. Instead, a trained mind required years of hard study to meet the needs of the people, and full preparation included a spiritual focus as well as knowledge. This meant a complete surrender to the work neither ignoring the role of the Holy Spirit nor relying on him to fill gaps in preparation of the ministry. The latter was an explicit rejection of what some called "blind inspiration," meaning a complete avoidance of any preparation of messages while supposedly relying on the Spirit for guidance. Instead, L.W. urged pastors to: "Trust God as if everything depended on him; work as if everything depended on you."

Marks also sought "a heart for everybody's woes, a remedy for every wrong," and recognition of every good. He wanted to be knowledgeable in matters that concerned his congregation from "setting hens to matrimonial ventures" and to guard confidences with confidence and always be prepared to respond to the call for either a wedding or a funeral. Finally, a pastor's preaching would always be focused on Jesus and drawn from a wide range of biblical resources. "Gather the people about St. Simon. Visit the plains of Abraham. Call on Jacob. Go down to Egypt with Joseph, climb the mountain heights with St. Isaiah, journey about Galilee and Jordan. Follow Paul in his missionary journey. Stand with John on Patmos." [43]

Another message reflected his expectation of the church. Using II Peter 3:1 and Philippians 3:13 as texts, he called for the church to treat the pastor as a brother and not a hired man; support him and join with him in the work of the church; not expect opinions or entertainment; receive him and treat him as a shepherd; trust him and confide in him. [44]

These ideas were also reflected in his focus on what he called "the business side." He urged thought, prayer, and regular attendance at worship and business meetings. He strongly enjoined each family to adopt a system for giving by either setting aside a certain percent or budgeting a fixed amount to be paid periodically. He defended his belief that the first method was preferable but did not argue for it exclusively nor did he specify a ten percent figure for a tithe. He also did not expect all of a family's giving to go to the local church, encouraging regular support as well as special offerings for missions.

In many respects, the problems Marks faced in 1900 and throughout his ministry pointed to larger questions faced by Baptist progressives generally. Besides the suspicions they encountered about their credentials, emphases and methods, they were also unable to produce the immediate results associated with the revivalists of that time. Sid Williams and more notable examples such as Dwight L. Moody thus implicitly challenged many of the assumptions of the progressives who linked education and cooperation with the work of God. In turn, Marks and other progressives generally were unwilling to repudiate the revivalist heritage of the Great Awakening and its contemporary expressions. Likewise, they retained a mythology of the rural church that saw it as the primary vehicle for God's work. This left them in the contradictory position of defending techniques and institutions that frequently contradicted or opposed their own agenda. Such conflicts explain the ultimate supplanting of progressive leadership and would also limit Marks' personal success in the ministry.

In ensuing years, the disappointments that attended his pursuit of larger ministry opportunities in individual churches pushed him to accelerate his efforts in associational, newspaper, and other regional or state Baptist efforts. At the same time, his commitments and pastoral skills would ensure consistent successes among the churches he ministered to. He would often be disappointed but he never abandoned either his progressive convictions or his faith. In 1900, he soon buckled down to minister to the churches of rural Missouri. By fall, he had assumed duties at Wayland and Wyaconda churches and began a schedule of regular revivals while still seeking a church that could pay him for full-time work.

Besides the continuing issue of irregular payments, frequent changes in his arrangements with other churches often disrupted either finances or scheduling. His diaries reflect receiving calls from one church only to have it rejected the next week, being voted out at an annual meeting, only to be called again a month later and similar disruptions of his work. In another instance, he agreed to help a church out without consideration of salary, but they indicated they wanted to hear him first and then never followed up on his offer. On some occasions, these patterns reflected the work of individuals within the congregations who opposed the kinds of programs and ideas Marks advocated. In other instances, it was merely the old practice that favored annual replacement of pastors.[45]

By the end of the new year, he reported a total income of $314.30 from the Wyaconda Association and four churches plus revival offerings. He had also established relative stability with a schedule rotating between Wyaconda, Liberty, Monticello, and Mt. Salem Churches. Despite occasional disruptions, this basic arrangement persisted through most of 1901 during which time he earned a total of $814.47. He reported expenses of $821.45 in the same period, but that undoubtedly included service on his educational debts though they still amounted to $400.00 at year's end. That burden of responsibility increased during the year when John Higbie, who still held one of L.W.s notes, faced a financial crisis, probably as a result of crop failure in conjunction with a severe drought. At the same time, he reported receivables of $29.05 yet to be paid by the churches he pastored.[46]

L. W.'s preaching schedule and events during a four-month period in 1901 give some picture of the rigors faced by rural preachers at the time. In January, he preached on one Saturday and Sunday at Liberty, Mt. Salem, and Monticello, plus two sundays at Wyaconda and held a two-week revival at New Woodville. The next month he followed the same weekly schedule plus an additional Saturday at Wyaconda and one service at New Woodville. In March, he preached twice at each church except Liberty where only one service was held. There were only slight variations in the schedule for the rest of the year.

Significantly, he never missed a service for any of these congregations during this period despite regular reports of adverse weather and "frightful" roads. He also reported at least two bouts with severe neck pain, requiring two visits to a physician, rare occurrences in the Marks' household. He finally missed a scheduled service at one church in December indicating he was too ill to preach; the day before he reported temperatures at 18 below zero.

The next twelve months produced continuing gains at all of his churches, most notably at Wyaconda. He was pleased with the growth of the Sunday school and missions support there, and the church began construction of a new building during the summer of 1901. He had been urging that action for some time, and the church finally voted 14-4 in favor that June despite the opposition of one committee member. By the end of the month, the membership had pledged $355.00, and work began on the foundation in August. He dug the space for the baptistery to be located below the speaker's platform in September. Marks declared the church "a real beauty" and preached the first sermon in the new building the last Sunday in November. By this time, most of the costs for the building had been pledged.[47]

He then faced a surprising church decision to hire another pastor. Only twenty-four had been in attendance when the question was called, and fourteen had voted to call J. A. Minter. The move had been made in response to one deacon's agitation and was a surprise to the rest of the congregation as well as Minter, who later reported he was not available. Marks indicated the membership was shocked and decided to "try to keep quiet and wait developments." That strategy seemed to work as he soon reported a great reaction against the vote. "Those who did it have brought down a storm on their heads . . . I trust the Lord will forgive them." The vote was finally rescinded, and L. W. reported a "fine spirit" by February.[48]

The addition of nineteen new members including nine baptisms later that month confirmed his assessment. Those results together with continuing strong attendance at a Thursday evening Bible study he initiated probably explain his rejection of a query from a St. Joseph Church that March and his purchase of a home site in Wyaconda. He would reconsider later in the year by which time he was beginning to show signs of restlessness as he joined a lodge and began to participate in local politics.

Some time prior to 1901, L. W. had joined the local chapter of the International Order of Odd Fellows. His log indicated both increasing commitment and corresponding satisfaction with the lodge during the next two years. He derived considerable satisfaction from his advancement to leadership in the lodge. He reported "unanimous" election to varied offices in 1901-02 with noticeable pride and always noted if he missed the regular Tuesday night meeting. As many progressives, Marks saw lodges as a complementary force for the work of the church because of their focus on social and material needs in contrast to the church's primary emphasis on the spiritual. Some people even expected lodges to function as the applied arm of Christianity. He was careful to distinguish between the two, however, and always stressed the superior role of the church.[49] It is also apparent he enjoyed the kind of fellowship the lodge offered as it represented opportunity to move beyond the immediate confines of the church body and inherent restrictions on his association there. He could fellowship without being accused of favoritism or independent of whatever pressing issue faced at any give time by the church.

Marks had occasionally referred to state political events while at the seminary and on his return to Missouri. The few references give only slight indications of his thought on partisan issues, though some aspect of the progressive spirit showed. His complete lack of references to national issues reveals a person whose mind as well as heart was oriented to the state and local. Still, his diaries alone would not have prepared a reader for the flurry of political interest that began in March 1902. This came when the prohibition question reached Lewis County.

His first reference to the prohibition issue noted that he had prevailed in an argument with a "wet," a proponent of open saloons. Most religious groups had taught temperance historically, but temperance was relatively new as a mainstream position. It emerged in conjunction with a wing of the social gospel movement that sought to stamp out evils affecting families and problems attending alcohol abuse. Much of the progressive reform impetus derived from the social gospel's mandate to address the needs of the poor. It did not require a giant step from that goal to attacks on alcohol abuse and from these to efforts to regulate or eliminate its availability. In addition, there were strong precedents for moral proclamations against drunkenness in Christian teaching generally, and it did not need a giant step to carry those convictions into the political arenas of a burgeoning democracy.

The moral imperative reached its apex in the latter stages of the national progressive movement as seen in the enactment of prohibition in 1918. Decades before, those values were widely distributed across small town America where there was the added dimension of community values and concern for neighbors long before they reached the national level. Thus, whatever the moral issue, small town churches and those of every size and denomination endorsed at least some aspects of the moral crusade.

By 1900, advocacy of prohibition had become a
hallmark of progressive Baptists, even though the
Southern Baptist Convention had yet to take a definitive
stand on the issue. Missouri would never enact statewide
prohibition but a series of laws had been passed by that
time mandating strict requirements for the location of
dram shops within communities. In accord with those
provisions, someone had evidently gathered the
appropriate number of signatures and requested
permission from the county to establish two dram shops,
presumably within the limits of Wyaconda.

Marks joined other drys in gathering signatures for a
petition opposing the request. A message he entitled "A
local option speech" probably dates from this campaign
and offers a sense of his approach to that issue. He made
five main points: church members had a duty to oppose
saloons; saloons are indefensible; their value as a revenue
source is a fallacy and the parallel idea that prohibition
kills the local economy can be disproved by countless local
examples such as Ft. Scott, Kansas and Aurora; it can be
enforced; and, "the onward sweep of prohibition is
irresistible. Today Missouri—tomorrow the nation. Note
the line up, and take your side." The issue became
increasingly divisive with some threats against those who
had signed the petitions. His political flurry ended with
the county court's decision to grant the licenses in April.[50]

Marks would also publicly support a water issue that
fall, but he was not particularly active in the campaign.
Nevertheless, his activities in Wyaconda established a
precedent for his work at future pastorates. Most of his
efforts in Lewis County and the surrounding area
consisted of helping churches organize or resolve
administrative problems. These were typical duties for an
employee of an association, but there is no evidence he

received any payment for these services. Almost certainly he was not paid for his work he did with area black congregations during this time. However, that work mirrored the broader associational commitments. The annual meeting of the Wyaconda Association often included time on the program for solicitation of funds on behalf of Macon College, a small college located at Macon largely supported by black Baptists. Black preachers might also preach at associational gatherings. Marks and others were especially impressed by one black preacher, James Hawkins, who delivered the only sermon Marks praised during the 1902 meeting.[51]

By 1901, Marks had also added yet another layer of work to the mix of his work. Progressive goals and regular financial needs fueled varied newspaper-related activities he began in that year and accelerated during the next two. He first reported distributing copies of the *Western Recorder* within the Wyaconda church in June 1901. He made no reference to selling subscriptions at that time and probably distributed the newspapers as a part of a general educational effort parallel to other promotions in the church. This time frame also connected closely with an article he wrote on lodges for *Word & Way*.

As 1902 progressed, Marks accelerated his work selling newspaper subscriptions in conjunction with his stated goal of debt reduction and a "good year's work for the Lord." The subscription sales offered the dual advantage of improving his income without interfering with his church-related work and was consistent with his belief in strengthening churches through information from newspapers. He first reported selling subscriptions in March of 1902 for *Central Baptist*. Five months later, S. M. Brown of *Word & Way* had to leave the Wyaconda Association meeting early and asked L. W. to solicit in his place. L. W. then gained nine subscriptions in addition to writing an account of the meeting for the newspaper. The next month he obtained about ten more subscriptions from the meeting of another association.[52]

At the same meeting, L. W. led the effort to raise funds to reduce the debt for LaGrange College. He then reported that the entire debt of $1,000 had been pledged. That success plus his subscription sales drew the attention of S. M. Brown who was in aggressive pursuit of broadened markets for the *Word & Way*. In October, he met with L. W. during the meeting of the General Association at St. Louis. He then asked L. W. to be field editor for *Word & Way*. Marks promised to think it over but deemed the offer "a mighty big thing for me to undertake." Shortly thereafter, he was invited to preach at Blackwell, Oklahoma in view of a call to conduct a revival at nearby Pond Creek.[53]

Events during the next three months caused him to give even more attention to the offer from *Word & Way*. The Mt. Salem Church voted to first rescind his call then overturned that action even as they continued contacting preachers whom they could hire cheaper than Marks. Under these circumstances, Marks preached a final sermon and withdrew his name from consideration. He then received a letter from a small church nearby which he offered to help at little or no cost because they were struggling to continue. They wrote back that they wanted to hear him first. L. W. responded to that rejection with "So it goes." [54]

His experiences with the horses he needed for local transportation added to his frustration. He bought a team of matched ponies, but they were not well trained, and their antics and road problems probably explain a serious buggy wreck he had earlier in the year. Related events for the rest of the year approached low comedy. Although he liked the ponies' appearance, they continued to bolt. For one reason or another, he finally traded them for a mare. She was gentler but still a fast trotter and did not turn out as well as he had expected, so he sold her and bought another team. By October, he was trying to sell the mare from that brace as she had started kicking. He finally obtained yet another team at the end of the month. He had profited at some stages during all of this trading but ultimately lost some of his hard gained money. Such stories help to explain why one family member would later comment that "Pop always gave boot." In fact, however, his other efforts with his stock, including both pigs and cattle, did much to help stretch the family's meager resources.[55]

L. W. faced most of the difficulties he encountered with equanimity whether in the pastorate or less significant matters such as his horses; he would note the problem in his diary and then return to work rarely reflecting any continuing agitation.   In contrast, renewal of conflicts at Wyaconda in late 1902 troubled him deeply. He wrestled with the problems resulting from active opposition of the deacon who had led the abortive effort to dismiss Marks the previous year. Then in early December, the deacons announced their interest to delay consideration of his call. The next day, he decided to accept the offer from *Word & Way* to assume a position as field editor, though he still hoped to assume those duties while serving at Wyaconda and at least a few months longer at Monticello.[56]

On December 9, L. W. sent his proposal to the *Word & Way* offices. The next day he also contacted J. M. Hunt, a publisher of Baptist books, and began a revival at Mt. Salem. He obtained fourteen subscriptions plus three renewals before returning home the next week. His early return was in response to Sadie's request as all of the children were ill, yet he still managed to submit his first postings as field editor on the 20th.[52]

In the meantime, Marks preached a sermon dealing with his response to the deacons' calls for resignation. Marks avoided "naming names" and reflected a gracious acceptance of the church's action but also offered a direct challenge to those who had engineered the action. He first asserted that the votes, possibly 22 to 16 and 21 to 18, had not represented the voice of the church. He then went on to argue that the actions mirrored those that had taken place in the church previously and that this pattern showed something was "radically wrong." He argued that a "determined few" should not rule, and the only hope of the church was to break up the coalition.[58]

Any hope of reconciliation was destroyed in a stormy meeting the next week. His deacon-adversary had rallied his forces, and L. W. reported he "looked like the devil was in him bigger than anybody I ever saw." At the end of the meeting, L. W. had been replaced by another. Some of the members, nevertheless, held a Christmas dinner and brought presents for him and the family, but he felt as if his decision had been made for him. On Christmas, he wrote the Blackwell church agreeing to supply there and resigned at Liberty two days later to focus on work with the *Word & Way*.[59]

1. *A History of the Baptists* 20; *The Southern Baptist Convention* 136-138; *Baptist Succession* 44-52; *The Baptist Heritage* 50, 445-447, 453, 457-58; E. Glenn Henson, "Between Two Worlds: Southern Seminary, Southern Baptists and American Theological Education," *Baptist History and Heritage* 20, #2: 28-33; Yarbrough, Slayden, "Academic Freedom and Southern Baptist History," *Baptist History and Heritage* 39, #1: 43-46; Mike Williams, Glenn Jonas, and Rosalie Beck, "100 Years after the Whitsitt Controversy," and "The Role of B. H. Carroll: A Panel Discussion," *Baptist History and Heritage*, 33, #3, (Autumn 1998) 30.

2. Marks' diaries, January 1, 1898; the diary for 1904 is missing and there may be others lost from before 1898.

3. Marks' diaries, January–February 1898, passim.

4. Marks' diaries, January–February 1898, passim.

5. Marks' diaries, January-April 1899, passim.

6. Marks' diaries, April 1899, passim.

7. Marks' diaries, August 1899 and November 20, 1899, passim.

8. Marks' diaries, December 1898 and June, July, and August 1899, passim.

9. Ibid

10. Marks' diaries, July–August 20, 1899, passim.

11. Marks' diaries, September 13 and October 12, 1898; October 10, 1899, undated note at end pages in 1899 diary.

12. Marks' diaries, June 29, July 2, 7, 8, 9-18 and November 3 1898.

13. Undated ca. August 1898 unidentified newspaper clipping, Marks miscellaneous files; Marks' diaries, July 2, August 29, September 1, and November 1, 1898, and July 23 and August 25, 1899.

14. Marks' diaries, September 1-29, 1899, passim.

15. Marks' diaries, September 29, 1899.

16 Marks' diaries, January 13, 1899 and May 5, 1898.

17. *The Baptist Heritage* 434-446, passim; *The Southern Baptist Convention* 135; and Paul Harvey, "Southern Baptists and the Social Gospel," 64-65.

18. Marks' diaries, December 23, and January 10, 1899.

19. Marks' diaries, January 6, 1898; the traducian theory asserts that the soul is a part of the inherited identity of human beings.

20. Marks' diaries, August 13, 15 and 18, 1898.

21. Ibid

22. Marks' diaries, November 12-13, 1899 and March 23, 1900.

23. Marks' diaries, February 6 and March 15, 1900.

24. Marks' diaries, December 20 and 26, 1899 and May 18, 1900.

25. Marks' diaries, April 30, 1900.

26. Marks' diaries, March 19, 1900.

27. Marks' diaries, January 7, February 23, May 5-12, and 14-16, and October 7, 1898 and June 1, 1899.

28. *The Southern Baptist Convention* 133-136.

29. Ibid; *The Baptist Heritage* 418, 422-423, and 446; Dan Gentry, "The Saint's Suitor," *Baptist History and Heritage,* v. 30, #3, Winter 2003: 7-25.

30. *The Southern Baptist Convention* 133-136; *The Baptist Heritage* 418, 422-423, and 446; "The Saint's Suitor" 7-25.

31. *The Baptist Heritage* 434-446, passim; William H. Whitsitt, *A Question of Baptist History,* (Louisville, KY: Cha's T. Dearing, 1896) 6 and passim; W. O. Carver, "William Heth Whitsitt: The Seminary's Martyr," *The Review and Expositor,* October 1954: 449-469; Rufus W. Weaver, "Life And Times of William Heth Whitsitt," *The Review and Expositor,* April 1940: 115-132; and E. B. Pollard, "The Life And Work of William Heth Whitsitt, *The Review and Expositor,* April 1912: 159-184; *Western Recorder,* May 5, 1897; and Leon McBeth, *Resources for Baptist History* (Nashville, TN: Broadman Press, 1990) 315-316.

32. Marks' diaries, October 7, 1898 and undated last page of 1899.

33. *Western Recorder,* May 6 and 27, 1897 and September 23, 1897; *Texas Baptist Standard,* August 19, 1897; Marks' diaries, August 19, 1897 and January 7, 1898.

34. Marks' diaries, April 7, 1898.

35. Marks' diaries, May 6, 1898; *Western Recorder,* May 6, 1898.

36. Marks' diaries, July 18, 1898; *Catalog* (Southern Baptist Theological Seminary, 1900) 16.

37. Marks' diaries, May 12 and 13, 1899.

38. Marks' diaries, June 1 and October 16, 1899.

39. Marks' diaries, September 5, 17, 18, and 29, 1899.

40. Marks' diaries, October 2-3, 1899.

41. Marks' diaries, February 19 and 24, March 4, 5, 12, 15, 22, and 3, April 2 and 14, May 19, 1900.

42. Marks diaries April 14, 1900.

43. Sermon files, Marks Collection.

44. Ibid.

45. Marks' diaries, December 14, 1901, October 11 and November 9 and 25, 1902.

46. Marks' diaries, end of year summaries for 1900 and 1901.

47. Marks' diaries, May 16, June 14 and 15, August 19, September 6, and October 19, 1901.

48. Marks' diaries,, January 18, February 16, and December 14, 22, and 31 1902.

49. Undated message entitled "M.W.A."; Sermon files, Marks Collection.

50. Ibid; Marks diaries March 31, April 21-28 and May 2, 1902.

51. Marks' diaries, August 30, 1902.

52. Marks' diaries, March 3 and August 20-22, 1902.

53. Marks' diaries September 24 and October 20-23, 1902.

54. Marks diaries November 25, 27-28 and December 6-7, 1902.

55. Marks' diaries, January 2, February 16, April w5, May 15-16, July 7-8, October 10, 29 and 30 1902. March 3, August 20-22, September 24 and October 20-23 and 26, 1902.

56. Marks' diaries, November 25, 27, 28 and December 6-7 1902.

57. Marks' diaries, December 9-12 and, 15 1902.

58. Marks' diaries, December 22 and 27 1902 and untitled, undated sermon, Sermon files, Marks Collection. Archives.

59. Marks diaries December 22 and 25 1902.

CHAPTER 3

Oklahoma and *The Word & Way*

L. W.'s initial purpose for going to Oklahoma was to conduct a revival and explore the possibility of securing a call to a new pastorate. He also intended to sell subscriptions for *Word & Way* while exploring wider possibilities for the newspaper there. This should have meant two weeks at most, but he would find it difficult to leave or to stay away once he returned to Missouri. The Pond Creek revival lasted much longer than he expected and circumstances and his heart would soon pull him back to the emerging state.

Marks was drawn to Oklahoma primarily because the idea of a frontier stimulated both his dreams and plans. He had probably contributed to a fund for territorial relief almost eight years before and had explored preaching opportunities there before settling in at Wyaconda in 1900. He shared the view of many who regarded the area as the last frontier where the nation fulfilled its manifest destiny. It also provided the stage where one such as L. W. Marks could hope to foster a new work carrying his vision to new lands, planting the seeds of his ideas in unplowed ground.

Events and his early successes there would add to his hopes. His beloved Aunt Ran had moved to the territory a few years before to join her children, and part of Sadie's family had settled near Blackwell. He also found others from Missouri throughout northern Oklahoma as natives of that state formed the largest cohort of the territory's population, numbering 43,589 of 313,900 in 1900.[1]

He regularly rhapsodized over the beauty of the country around Blackwell and Pond Creek describing it as some of the finest country "I ever saw." He was especially impressed with Blackwell which he portrayed as filled with enterprising people. Among that number were at least twenty-nine Missourians who welcomed him to the Blackwell church and attended a dinner there after he had taught Sunday school and preached there the first Sunday in January. He reported a favorable impression from the congregation and expressed an interest in serving as pastor but did not push his candidacy. The previous pastor had departed some time earlier, and the church had struggled during and after his pastorate. L. W. began a revival the next day at nearby Pond Creek that continued for much of the next three weeks, finally closing on the 25th. There were at least nine decisions during this time among which seven were baptized. He reported his delight with an offering of $23.30 which he regarded as "great for the little church."[2]

He was equally pleased with results from sales of *Word & Way*, obtaining at least seventy-five subscriptions at Blackwell, Pond Creek, Enid, Kingfisher, El Reno, Yukon, and Shawnee during the month. He preached both services at Shawnee the first Sunday in February and then began extended meetings at nearby Tecumseh. He saw the opportunity for a good work there but was torn by his desire to help meet that need and the call of home. His own longings for family time were compounded by a letter from Sadie encouraging him to return as soon as possible, so he protested the church's vote for an extended meeting. Once the church decided to continue the meeting, he wrote: "I could have died. I am so homesick, but I will try to do the Lord's will." Eight additions and an elated pastor were compensation, but he also had to face tensions within the church. Marks regarded the pastor as a "good man" but counseled him and suggested that he ought to resign because of his part in the church problems.[3]

He finally closed the Tecumseh meeting and then traveled to Norman and Oklahoma City to sell *Word & Way* subscriptions. On February 11, he met with L. L. Smith, the corresponding secretary of the Oklahoma Baptist State Convention, the Baptist association that coordinated both Northern and Southern Baptist missionary efforts in Oklahoma Territory. Smith greeted Marks "heartily" and urged him to consider locating in Oklahoma City and editing an Oklahoma department of *Word & Way*. Smith's proposal was endorsed by W. W. Anderson of the First Baptist Church of that "rushing city." Marks liked the idea and shared it with *Word & Way* management the next day in Kansas City. They objected, arguing that Marks was "so badly needed in Missouri." The paper was about to merge with the Central Baptist and wanted to launch a major sales campaign in Kansas City.[4]

Before that event began, Marks returned home for a week-long reunion with the family. While there, he reported the sale of his team of horses at some profit. He also reported attending services at Wyaconda but made no comments about the quality of the message delivered by his replacement. The rest of the month was spent between home and Kansas City when he conducted a "thorough canvas" with notable successes despite the fact *Word & Way* was not well known there.

Then on March 5, S. M. Brown told him of a change of plans at the paper. They had purchased the *Indian*

Territory Baptist and now wanted Marks to do an Oklahoma department with the eventual goal of combining Indian and Oklahoma Territory work. He agreed two days later to an arrangement that provided him a salary of $1,000 annually plus expenses to be taken from fifty percent of the revenue he gained for the paper in the Territory. The paper also agreed to offset half of his losses if he fell short of that goal and assured him of a position with the firm in Missouri offices if the Oklahoma venture didn't work out.

Two days later he decided to go. He completed the Kansas City sales campaign and returned home to pack up and sell out. Sadie and the children then joined her Freeman relatives near Memphis, Missouri. He arrived in Oklahoma City on March 28, attending a service at the Independence Avenue Church in the morning and preaching for a different congregation that evening. L. W. Marks would now have the opportunity to test his ideas and implement his dreams.[5]

When L. W. moved to Oklahoma Territory in 1903, it was still frontier in many respects as was the adjacent Indian Territory to the east. Oklahoma Territory had only recently been settled in a series of land openings from the land run of 1889 to a giant land lottery in 1901, and one small portion was still unsettled. The Five Civilized Tribes had begun settlement of Indian Territory more than sixty years before, but there were still large areas of raw frontier in both territories. In sharp contrast, both Oklahoma City and Guthrie were relatively modern cities with populations of more than 10,000 people. And, all across the territories, railroads were promoting the development of new regions and towns almost daily. As a result, Indian Territory was poised to exceed 700,000, and Oklahoma Territory was approaching that number.

Those elements alone appealed to Marks, but he was drawn even more to the opportunity to shape Baptist institutions in the emerging state. In many respects, he and his co-workers accomplished that task and much more in ensuing years. Within ten years from the time of his arrival, Marks and his fellow Baptists would build strong foundations for the newspaper and educational efforts he believed in so strongly. The same decade would also see the establishment of an orphan's home, a rescue home for young women, and a general strengthening of churches. From building programs to improved Sunday schools and the spread of youth work, Baptists consolidated their institutions and continued to build. They were ultimately so successful that few people today recognize or appreciate the scope of their accomplishment attributing the Baptist preeminence in the state to the commitments that defined the settlers on arrival. In fact, territorial Baptist leaders and institutions shaped the state and its people despite inauspicious beginnings.

That statement may seem a surprising one about a state whose residents were seven times more likely to identify themselves as Baptists than more typical American population groups in 2000. Or, stated another way, Baptists represent slightly more than one-third of the population of the Sooner state with 967,223 adherents identified among the state's 2000 population of 3,450,854 people. Indeed, Oklahoma can claim to be the buckle of the Bible belt. The point is, however, that there was no guarantee that would occur when the state was in the process of formation, and the outcome was still unsettled in 1910, if not in 1920. A generation of Baptist leaders, with L. W. Marks often at the forefront and always as an active supporter and promoter, developed the programs that would give Oklahoma a singularly Baptist identity.[6]

The data supporting some of these arguments may be found in both U. S. Census and Baptist denominational reports. The Census of 1890 for Oklahoma Territory, taken shortly after the first land run, indicated about eight percent of the population were church members. They were distributed among nine Baptist, ten Congregational, seventeen Presbyterian, and fifty-one Methodist congregations. None of the Baptist congregations reported having a building at the time of the census. Homes, schools, and any other available buildings were used for worship purposes in the first year of settlement. There is even a tradition that the First Baptist Church of Oklahoma City held its initial meeting in a saloon. That body, located in the fastest growing city in the new territory, did not organize formally until November 2, 1889, more than six months after the land opening, and it was a little more than a year before the congregation's fifty-one members dedicated their first building.[7]

Even allowing for the fact Baptists do not count children among their membership until they have made a profession of faith and then been baptized, the experience of this church, which was already recognized as the leading Baptist congregation in the territory, would not suggest a foundation for shaping a state. And, Baptist prospects did not appear that much better in Indian Territory where Methodists outnumbered them almost two to one with 351 congregations reported vs. 181 for the Baptists who claimed only a few scattered buildings dedicated to exclusive use by churches.

By 1906, at the time of a special religious census, a different picture had emerged. Baptists had almost caught the Methodists with 27.1% of the population vs. 29.7%. The same census reported a total of 1,161 Baptist congregations of which 856 were aligned with the

Northern or Southern Baptist Convention, 305 black churches affiliated with the National Baptist Convention, and the remainder scattered among Freewill, General, and other Baptist groups. The same report indicated the Northern and Southern churches now had a total of 445 church buildings. By this time as well, First Baptist Church of Oklahoma City was recognized as one of the leading churches among all denominations in the territory.[8]

Some of this dramatic reversal could be attributed to a change in composition of the settlers from four land runs after 1889 and other demographic shifts, but it was also clearly the product of the work of Baptist organizational leaders and workers who built on two strengths while struggling against one major problem. Their first advantage lay in their combination of focus and energy. Although divided on many issues, the Baptists were determined to claim the state for Christianity and a Baptist version of that faith.

Marks was immediately taken by the evidence of Baptist energy and success. One of his first postings for the *Word & Way* depicted them as "driving like Jehu, launching a college, an orphan's home, a rescue home, sanitarium, and urban and Colportage ministries. He would regularly boast, "What progress these Baptists are making" and delight in the chance to bring his progressive values to bear on their institutions.[9]

Beyond their enthusiasm and determination, the Baptists' advantage lay in the flexibility characteristic of the congregational form of government. The rapid population of Oklahoma and Indian Territories overwhelmed available resources in most denominations. In contrast, Episcopalians did not manage to establish a bishopric for Oklahoma until 1895, well after both territories were largely settled. Similarly, Presbyterians regularly struggled to supply clergy to the churches they established, partly because of their insistence on educational standards for clergy. Thus, the Baptists' only real competition for dominance came from the Methodists.[10]

The Methodists held the initial advantage because they were better organized than the fragmented Baptists. Whereas both Methodists and Baptists were divided between northern and southern wings, the Baptists added a host of territorial divisions to the denominational mix. One part of this problem had been effectively addressed by 1900 with the formation of the Oklahoma Baptist State Convention for Oklahoma Territory (OBSC) and the Baptist General Convention of Indian Territory (GBICT), each in turn, cooperating with both the Southern and Northern Conventions. The two individuals who deserve the credit for most gain were L. L. Smith of Oklahoma and J. S. Murrow of Indian Territory. Each would also play major roles in L. W. Marks' career in Oklahoma.

Their achievement, however, resolved only some of the Baptist fragmentation as they were often diverted from larger goals by a tendency for doctrinal splitting and parochialism. The latter was especially detrimental to the support of institutions such as the children's home, colleges, and newspapers. Support for the home diminished with each additional mile separating a church from the home's location in Oklahoma City, and each region tended to want its own schools and newspapers. L. W. Marks would spend the better part of the next ten years of his life trying to reverse those tendencies.

L. W. arrived in Oklahoma City on March 29, 1903, in time to attend the dedication of the Independence Avenue Church and then to preach that evening at Michigan

Avenue. The next day he mailed copies of the *Word & Way* to all the pastors of Oklahoma together with a letter. In the next weeks, he began regular meetings with the state mission board and participated in the formation of a weekly meeting of Oklahoma City area Baptist ministers.

He spent weeks searching for a house he could afford but soon reported he was "tired and disgusted" at purchase of rental prices typical in the growing city. He hoped to buy one house from L. L. Smith for $1,550 but was unable to gain financing. He finally found a house he could afford on 7th Street and celebrated the arrival of his family on April 29. Four days later he began his work outside Oklahoma City.[11]

Marks' appointment as field editor for the *Word & Way* was announced on the first page in the April 2, 1903 issue of that publication. The editors identified their goal as becoming "the medium of communication for our Oklahoma brethren." Toward that end, they were creating an Oklahoma Department to report matters of denominational interest from across the territories. They went on to praise Marks as "one of the best of men, a conservative, wise, industrious, educated man . . . strong with his pen, strong in the pulpit, compassionate and brotherly . . . a counselor and helper." Marks' "Salutary" introduced his column, echoed the editors' goals, and defined the commitments that would define his work and justify their praise. He identified his purpose as service to every department of the Baptist work that is clearly for the advancement of "the Bible, the Home, and the Church." He concluded his article with a pledge to become an integral part of Baptist forces.[12]

His greeting also affirmed his continuing commitment to progressive goals and emphases. In this instance, that meant pursuing "the things that made for peace among the brethren (and) fighting the common enemy . . . " to building Baptist forces in the territory. He would later compliment the churches of Oklahoma for their commitment to cooperation and harmony, characterizing it as the "Oklahoma Way." He indicated Baptists in other states could learn from the Oklahoma example and regarded the quality as something that all should be humbly grateful for. In contrast, he noted: "Now and then we meet a brother who feels called to straighten out all the kinks in his brethren and hold the denomination to the line . . . but his sphere of work is usually confined to a small area." Such doctrinal brethren were "mostly backbone and bustle" and inclined to measure their success by the number of people they had made mad. "They are great on baptism, communion, succession, etc. but a little shy on mission."[13]

Marks' perception of Baptist work in Oklahoma was based on wide exposure to ministers and churches across both Oklahoma and Indian Territories. The second territory was added to his assignment in July after the *Word & Way* completed purchase of the *Indian Territory Baptist* and its subscription list. S. M. Brown apparently told Marks that there were 3,000 subscribers to that paper, but that is highly unlikely as there is no evidence extant of the paper, and no such periodical was supported by any of the mission groups active in Indian Territory. Even if the paper had been well known, that would have been an excessive number. The *Word & Way* claimed only 723 subscribers in Indian Territory in April 1903, and Marks had gained more than 200 of those in the short time he had spent in the territory.[14]

L. W. 's basic pattern of work in both Oklahoma and Indian Territory was much the same as he had employed in Missouri while at Wyaconda. This meant attending association meetings to promote the newspaper in direct sales, seeking endorsements of associations, and developing a network of contacts. He would also frequently go to the individual churches of an association and sell directly to the membership. Quite often that schedule included Sunday or other dates set aside by the full church. Most ministers supported such efforts, including some who were not advocates of the *Word & Way*. For example, the pastor at Ada supported the *Western Recorder* but nevertheless helped Marks develop a list for a systematic canvas of that community.[11]

Regular supply and revival preaching added to his opportunities to promote the *Word & Way* while also offsetting some of his expenses. On the other hand, there is also a suggestion from his notes that his employment with *Word & Way* may have been seen by some congregations as an excuse for offering fair compensation for his work. His appearance may have contributed to that as he believed in professional appearance. Always noted for his cleanliness and neat appearance, he may have projected a level of prosperity and thus less need for support.

When combined with a pattern of slow payment from *Word & Way* offices and his frequent inability to collect on subscription pledges, those factors meant he still faced regular financial pressures. Usually Marks accepted church offers at whatever level without complaint. He noted, for example, one pastor was a bit disappointed that an offering for a week-long meeting at Ralston gained only $22.40, but L. W. made no judgment call of his own. Two exceptions to that rule occurred at Guthrie and at Chandler. After preaching at that territorial capital church, Marks lamented the lack of an invitation to stay in a home and that he was given only a $4.00 offering, an amount that barely covered his $2.00 hotel bill. Nevertheless, he returned to that church on numerous occasions; a few months later they gave a $5.00 offering. He was even more upset by a $12.25 offering after a three-week meeting at Chandler, especially since it occurred in the weeks preceding Christmas when he was beginning to worry about being able to afford gifts for his family.[16]

Marks undoubtedly held an accurate sense of what a church could have afforded to pay him. He had also learned then from his own experience that some churches had traditions of paying any minister as little as possible. Undoubtedly, some of the churches who were shorting him were behind in their payments to their pastors, which meant pastors were often reluctant to spur giving. In contrast, to occasional complaints about compensation for churches, he never complained about the hardships that often went with the hospitality offered by settlers in rural Oklahoma. He reported on staying in a soddy without comment. On other occasions, he would describe accommodations as fearful and breakfast as "sorry" but also noted the folks had "done the best they could."[17]

L.W. made every effort to be objective in both his personal diary and in his reporting about Baptist work. This meant he identified problems as well as strengths, but the gist of his reports point to dramatic growth at virtually every location in Oklahoma. These included areas such as northwest Oklahoma's Mt. Zion Association which had only ten churches and three pastors serving the association in 1903 . . . One source reporting from this area indicated his amazement to find a family who had never heard of Jesus. Many such families and others were living in sod houses and "dugouts."[18]

The Baptists used diverse means to reach the unconverted and to reenlist those Marks called "trunk babtists, spelled with two small b's," This was his term for those who had previously been members of a church in their home states but kept their letter of transfer in the trunk rather than join a local church. Many of the towns utilized Colportage ministries, distribution of religious pamphlets by wagon or rail, provided by the American Baptist publication society. The most prominent and the longest enduring efforts of that form of ministry persisted in the Oklahoma City area for at least ten years. Rev. L. H. Holt was in charge of the wagon and traveled through the country giving away Bibles, books, and gospel tracts. He also assisted in organizing churches and Sunday schools as opportunities arose. Others employed a railroad car designated as a chapel car which was moved from one site to another along the expanding railroad lines of the state. [19]

Marks attributed significant impact to these programs, but the most important tool Baptists utilized was extended meetings or revivals. The revivals were usually hosted by small local churches with assistance from an association, often with speakers from varied territorial Baptist offices. The impact of this process was often dramatic. For instance, the Northwest Association formed in the Woodward area in 1902 with nine churches. Ten new churches were recorded in the next year after a rush of settlement brought dozens of new families to the area with seventy-two new land claims filed in August 1903. One of the many churches organized during that time was at Pleasant View which started in December 1902 with nine members and had grown to thirty-nine by six months later. Another pastor in the area reported baptizing thirty-five people in the year, and this was without a protracted meeting.[20]

In October 1903, L. W. conducted a prolonged meeting at a small church fifteen miles south of Woodward. B. A. Loving, a pastor from nearby Persimmon, also preached some services. The church had been organized the year before but had been very slow to develop. The revival culminated November 8 with twenty-four baptisms in a nearby lake. Marks and Loving conducted the baptisms together, one standing on one side of each convert as they immersed them.

At other times, Marks celebrated the great power "of the Lord's presence" and reported a number of services where people wept, and some of the "wickedest men in the country were converted."[21] He filled his column with similar news from associations across the twin territories but reported even more dramatic numbers from the rapid growth of churches in Oklahoma City and other more populated areas of the new territory. The urban areas benefitted from continuing population growth and corresponding prosperity plus a concentration of institutions and resources. In central Oklahoma, the work of the Central Baptist Association added to the impact of the dynamic churches and leaders in the Oklahoma City area. The results of these efforts were both immediate and dramatic. In 1902, the OBSC alone reported an addition of 1,178 members and 2,435 baptisms of which 815 were conducted by associational missionaries. Similar growth the next year swelled Baptist ranks to 14,361 at the end of 1903, and the pace continued through the decade.[22]

The growth and missionary efforts of the First Baptist Church of Oklahoma City in this period illustrate part of that dynamic. Oklahoma City's growth had lagged following the depression of 1893, but the city soon continued its expansion toward status as the leading city in the two territories. Its primary rival in Oklahoma

Territory was Guthrie, but the territorial capital lost whatever long-term potential it held when the Frisco Railroad moved west from the area of present day to a railhead at Oklahoma City in 1897. The return of agricultural prosperity to outlying regions at the same time soon made it the fastest growing city in the nation, swelling from 4,000 to 64,000 between 1897 and 1910 with the First Baptist Church justly claiming to be the fastest growing church in the bustling city. In turn, its members, prosperity, and vision translated into significant evangelistic efforts throughout the city and territory.

Between 1895 and 1905, First Baptist Church sponsored six missions in the Oklahoma City area of which five became churches. First known as Southside Mission, Washington Avenue gained church status in 1901. Capitol Hill, established in 1897, followed the next year with Immanuel and then Olivet established in 1905. Then, the newer congregations often sponsored mission efforts of their own. For instance, in July 1903, Marks reported that Capitol Hill had begun a rural mission together with El Reno. At the same time, Washington Avenue was planning to sponsor another congregation.[23]

Marks joined Washington Avenue shortly after moving to the city. He often served as supply preacher in the absence of pastor J. A. Scott, a fellow graduate of Southern, and conducted one of the first deacon ordinations in the new church. More important, and closer to Marks' heart, his association with that church tied him to the establishment of the Oklahoma Baptist Children's Home. The year before Marks' arrival, Scott had introduced a resolution to that effect at the urging of his wife, Theodocia. The OBSC endorsed the resolution heartily, and the next year, the Indian Territory Convention approved a resolution as well, marking the first significant point of cooperation between the conventions of the two territories.

Scott was then elected superintendent while Mrs. Scott focused on gathering necessary supplies and raising funds. By the time Marks arrived in Oklahoma City, the home had grown to accommodate nine children. He and Sadie were frequent visitors at the home while L. W. regularly represented the home at association meetings in the two territories. His fund-raising efforts on behalf of the home were surpassed only by those of Scott; both of their labors were augmented by Marks' promotion of the home's needs in *Word & Way*. These contributions and others L. W. would make in ensuing years explain why J. M. Gaskin called L. W. one of the key figures who kept the home afloat in its early years.[24]

Marks travels with *Word & Way* and his own commitments also led him to considerable work on behalf of Sunday school conventions, the Baptist Young Peoples Union (BYPU), and early efforts in extension training for ministers. Neither Sunday school nor BYPU programs were unified in most churches at the time. Sunday schools had gained wide acceptance; though, many churches still did not have them or they were maintained primarily for young people. L. W. consistently spoke for Sunday schools in meetings of the Central Association and was a frequent speaker at Sunday school conventions which were often held in conjunction with association meetings.

The BYPU was even less well established than Sunday schools partly because it focused on training of Baptist youth; it would later be adapted for adults as well. Both Sunday schools and training unions had beginnings in the 1840s and gained prominence after the Civil War. Each began as interdenominational programs in urban areas where Sunday schools were frequently linked with general efforts to improve education for the masses and soon gained recognition as an evangelistic outreach tool as well. Although never presented that way, in the early years, Sunday schools tended to be for those outside the church who would hopefully be won to the church. The Southern Baptist Convention established a Sunday School Board in 1891 and began training programs shortly thereafter.[25]

Marks embraced the BYPU from his earliest contacts with it in Missouri and throughout his years in Oklahoma even as the BYPU was still struggling to develop bases of support. W. M. Anderson of First Baptist Church of Oklahoma City also promoted the cause in a publication he circulated during 1903 called the *Assistant Pastor*. This publication was apparently intended to complement the efforts of the pastoral conference. E. E. "Hot Dog" Lee became territorial organizer for the fledgling organization that year. In December 1903, the Southwest BYPU rally convened at Hobart. As had occurred with other associational rallies that year, the program did not draw the attendance hoped for. The meeting elected Rev. W. D. Moore of Anadarko as president of the association with the goal of linking BYPU organizations in the territory. Another beginning took place early the next year when Marks reported a proposal from a group of Kansas churches for a joint association with the Baptist young people of Oklahoma. Marks' commitment and contributions to these efforts would continue during subsequent years.[26]

The proposed linkage may also have been triggered by an institute Marks held at Oklahoma Baptist College in Blackwell in June 1903. The institute offered courses in basic Bible instruction along with instruction in sermon preparation and related areas to strengthen the skills and knowledge of area preachers. Marks was one of the

instructors and then elected president of the Oklahoma
Baptist Institute which was then formed to offer a similar
program annually.

By this time, Marks had already begun to focus much
of his energies on the promotion of Oklahoma Baptist
College.[27] The first meeting of the OBSC in October 1899
had called for and approved a recommendation to begin
work toward a college by establishing a goal of raising
$10,000 toward that end by the next April. A number of
towns competed for the honor to host the new college
with Noble offering a site for a campus and $4,000.
Blackwell interests made a better offer committing a site
and $5,000 in pledges to the effort.

Correspondingly, a board of trustees appointed and
formally organized on October 7, 1899. In December, the
board accepted the Blackwell proposal that now included
a donation of twenty acres and $15,000 toward building
costs. A building committee was established to oversee
construction of a building.[28] The college began offering
classes in September 1901 with fifty students and four
faculty members. Delegates to the OBSC meeting at Enid
journeyed by train to Blackwell for a formal dedication of
the building the following month.

A spirit of celebration attended these achievements
that seemed to justify the optimism of the delegates two
years earlier. At that time, they had emphasized the
importance of the college's establishment, celebrating the
expected impact of their achievement while contrasting it
with work in other states in a report from the convention:

> A very small percent of Baptists who have been
> educated by state universities have ever become efficient
> church workers. Our children must be educated under
> the influence of the Bible soundly interpreted. Nobody
> can do this for Baptists. We have ever stood in the
> forefront of educational progress, and we must do so in

> this territory. We have to this end begun a college at
> Blackwell, with a commodious building that is up-to-
> date in *every* appointment in its plans of structure. The
> prospects are bright before us. No state ever built such a
> college within twelve years of its founding, except
> Oklahoma.
>
> By educating our own ministry, we must elevate our
> standard of pulpit ability and church life. Experience
> teaches that in most instances preachers devote the best
> part of their lives to establishing the gospel in the state
> where they are educated. [29]

The Convention deserves credit for both its ambition
and its achievement, but the latter proved much more
difficult to sustain that to initiate. By the 1902 convention,
the college already faced a series of problems that would
eventually lead to its demise. Debts had accumulated
forcing reduction in faculty pay, and students would soon
begin an exodus to nearby Tonkawa, where the territorial
government had established a state prep school.

Marks was appointed to the Oklahoma Baptist College
board some time shortly after his arrival in Oklahoma.
That appointment aligned with both his commitments and
needs of the college. L. W. was quick to use the *Word &
Way* to promote the programs of the college and to
improve its financial standing. He was especially
concerned about fund-raising, urging "careful business-
like preparations" to raise money and to preserve a
"splendid college building" worth at least $40,000. In the
July 3rd issue of *Word & Way* he introduced a proposal
from Blackwell interests to address an "embarrassing"
$20,000 debt. The plan called for the Blackwell group to
assume one-half of that debt with Oklahoma Baptists to
commit to the remainder.

The college was also having difficulties locating a
president at that time, but a faculty member assumed
necessary duties, and the college opened on time in

September. In the meantime, Marks began fund-raising for the college at association meetings. He headed a special fund-raising effort at the Baptist State Convention in October and raised $1,400 to address a financial emergency, but no solution was found for the long-term debt. Marks was optimistic about additional pledges he obtained during the convention meeting in October and progress by Blackwell interests later that year, but 1903 ended with the debt unchanged. L.W. responded with an urgent plea in *Word and Way* calling for Baptist to unite in support of Baptist institutions. He argued that any other college would lead students away from Baptist principles and truths, but the debt problem persisted.[30]

Marks' work for the *Word & Way* plus his efforts for Oklahoma Baptist College gave him numerous occasions to promote values toward development of Baptists who were not "lopsided." He maintained his commitment to associational work for the same reasons. Associational work had defined the beginnings of Marks' career and would remain his one area of activity other than service to his local church long after he retired from an active ministry. He promoted associational work in a number of ways. He attended most of the annual meetings of the varied territorial associations, promoted them in *Word & Way* and was a frequent speaker on their programs. His most significant contributions, however, were in the Central Association and a consortium of Oklahoma City ministers.

Baptist ministers from the towns formed in the initial land run had cooperated in an association since that time. In April 1903, J. A. Scott, the pastor at Washington Avenue Baptist Church, hosted the first of a series of regular meetings of Oklahoma City area ministers. He and L. W. then wrote a constitution for a pastors' conference formed at that time. It initially had seven members who first agreed to meet weekly, but that proved incompatible with their schedules. In December, they began monthly meetings at which time they invited all interested pastors in the area to join them. Besides permitting quick unified responses to mission opportunities and coordination of revival campaigns, this body also formed a kind of executive committee for the Central Association.[31]

The Central Association was originally formed from churches from the original counties of Oklahoma Territory: Oklahoma, Logan, Lincoln, and Canadian. It soon grew to include a number of churches outside those borders as the territory expanded. By 1903, the association linked thirty-two churches and nineteen Sunday schools (usually a part of one of the churches), serving 2,500 people of whom about one-fourth were members at First Baptist Church, Oklahoma City. The prominence of that church, the participation of employees of the OBSC, and influential ministers such as J. A. Scott and Marks meant that this association frequently served as a driving force for the larger Oklahoma Baptist Convention.

As other associations in the territories, it also sponsored its own missionary program with at least one person on the field for a portion of most years. Despite relative prosperity, however, even this association struggled to fund its ministries. The August 1903 association meeting held at Washington Avenue Baptist church in Oklahoma City, for instance, reported on the work of missionary C. W. Morrison. He was owed $40.00 for his work and had been forced to abandon the field because of limited support.[32]

By the next year, Marks was one of three members of a special associational committee on Oklahoma territory missions. Their report affirmed the association held a "large portion of the responsibility for the success or failure of the mission work in Oklahoma Territory" and pledged "hearty support" to the effort to take the gospel to every community in Oklahoma. They also reported an improved financial picture for convention and association work, but elsewhere the association reported owing another missionary L. H. Holt $81.67 for five-months work.

Marks also began service that year as clerk-treasurer of the association, a position he would hold the next year and then with only one, two-year interruption from 1910-1925. The position primarily linked him to his fellow ministers in the Oklahoma City area and gave him a foundation for a significant role in state convention work. [33]

His first prominent role in the OBSC was directly connected to his work as editor of *Word & Way* and to his regular contacts with L. L. Smith. Their relationship had grown after Marks' location in Oklahoma City developed further in conjunction with mutual work in the pastor's conference and in the Central Association. Smith had been a driving force in the unification of territorial convention work and became the first corresponding secretary for the OBSC in 1901.

He and Marks shared similar commitments to cooperation, education, and newspapers as well as friendship. Smith addressed the 1903 association meetings with a stirring address on "Oklahoma for Christ and the Baptists," but he was already working against the advice of doctors and friends. He was already beginning to show signs of the illness that would soon take his life. Two months later, Marks would report Smith was "still sick." He went on to state that he was not dangerously ill but after another two weeks referred to a persistent fever and commented that Smith was sinking. He died November 22, an event that produced the first *Word & Way* headlines about Oklahoma matters. C.W. Brewer, a Norman attorney, was made corresponding secretary at a state mission board meeting, November 24, the date of Smith's funeral.[34]

Amid these changes, Marks was seeking alternatives to his employment with *Word & Way*. He had managed to secure endorsements for the paper from most of the territorial association and the BGSC. Before 1903, his primary competition was D. B. Ray's *Baptist Flag* and the *Western Baptist*, but a new paper emerged sometime during the year called the *Baptist Oklahoman*. Ray had preceded Marks into Oklahoma by at least three years. He had been active in the Central Association and had presided over the 1901 meeting and obtained an endorsement for the *Flag* the next year.[35] Ray became increasingly critical of territorial Baptist leadership during 1903, possibly as a response to competition from *Word & Way*. In June, L. W. noted that "The *Flag* is out and still nagging the *Word & Way*. I am receiving great commendation for not noticing him." Two weeks later, he noted, "Old Ben Ray of the *Flag* is on the warpath and after some of our leading brethren." The tactic backfired, and the Central Association refused to endorse the *Flag* at its July meeting despite Ray's pleading.[36]

The demise of the *Western Baptist* a few months later should have left the *Word & Way* in a dominant position especially since Marks had met the subscription goals defined by the front office. Yet, management at *Word & Way* had decided to reduce its commitment to Oklahoma at the end of the year. That contradictory action had at least two causes. The first stemmed from their overly optimistic projections about the Oklahoma market. The purchase of the Indian Territory newspaper left them with an investment they were unlikely to recover in the near future, and returns from the new subscriptions Marks generated were not keeping up with their costs. Part of that gap probably stemmed from their inability to collect on all the subscriptions he sold.[32]

Oklahoma was growing, but it was not growing rich. While Oklahoma City prospered, many small towns and rural villages still struggled as did farmers who were usually investing their yearly returns back into their farms. Moreover, a significant percentage of the rural population growth had been from sharecroppers and others who never approached the level of prosperity that would allow them to afford a newspaper of any kind, never mind a church publication. Those who did want a paper wanted one for their territory. The Baptist citizens of the twin territories also remained jealous of their respective jurisdictions, and the hope for separate statehood for each remained high for another two years after 1903.

In some respects, *Word & Way* was less appealing to such interests than other papers. The *Word & Way* was clearly a regional paper with columns for Kansas and Colorado, Oklahoma and Indian Territory, as well as its home state of Missouri where it had become the official state paper. Missourians, however, were not struggling to define their identities in the larger nation or even within Baptist work. Those issues had been settled for generations there while the people of the twin territories remained citizens of territories rather than states and thus especially sensitive to concerns about identity.

Marks had grown increasingly frustrated with *Word & Way* management as well. In October, he had lamented the paper's periodic failures to include most of the material he had submitted. Other diary notes reflected continuing cash flow problems. Some of this may have stemmed from the difference between his accounting of subscriptions sold and the home office's concern with payment received. Other payments also seemed to lag, however. On December 23, he lamented lack of money for either presents or obligations. There was no hope for donation to orphans, the rescue, or some extra cash for his mother. His end of year financial accounting defined his situation even more clearly. He reported income for the year of $857.57, almost a fifteen percent loss from his 1902 earnings.[38]

Word & Way's management also could not seem to grasp Marks' need for regular income to reimburse him for his expenses as well as to provide for the needs of his family. His diaries are full of comments about delays in payments, failure to compensate him for expenses and similar issues. Some of those delays could be explained by disagreements about the exact count of new subscriptions vs. renewals as well as periodic cash shortages at the home office. Nevertheless, it was evident he did not always receive payments when due.

Some of that disregard for Marks' financial needs may be explained two ways. First, management knew he also earned some income from pulpit supply and other preaching. Ironically, the reverse seemed to affect the income he earned from the churches he served. Marks was never averse to discussion of money matters and defending his interests. He would not, however, ever plead poverty. His appearance probably added to the impression of prosperity. One of the enduring memories for those who knew him was that he was always neat and well groomed.

A note from his *Word & Way* columns suggests another reason he was ready to reduce his commitment to *Word & Way*. After a prolonged stay at home, he wrote "We just keep going all day but land at the same place every night, and we have enjoyed sleeping in the same bed every night for a whole week. We hadn't had such an experience for most a year. We have slept in dugouts, tents, and shacks, fine homes and good hotels in depots and on trains. We have eaten of the fat of the land, also of the lean, combining the gifts of Jack Spratt and his wife."[39]

By December 1903, L. W. reached an agreement with the *Word & Way* office to continue his columns and sale efforts on a straight commission basis. The stated intention was for *Word & Way* to maintain a significant presence in Oklahoma but with reduced costs. In actuality, the move represented a practical abandonment of the Oklahoma field. L. W. would continue to write columns on an irregular basis in the future and sell subscriptions when possible. However, a decrease in Oklahoma coverage and declining sales efforts soon led to the disappearance of *Word & Way* subscriptions for all but its most loyal followers.

Before that event, Marks and his paper offered a voice of reasoned calm to the turmoil following the death of L. L. Smith and the *Flag* launched a scathing attack on the Oklahoma Baptist Convention leadership. Ray criticized the convention for a delay in printing the convention report, the appointment of C. W. Brewer, and especially Brewer's statement encouraging correspondence from ministers who might want to locate in Oklahoma. Brewer promised that he would "be ready at all times to assist in locating good men in Oklahoma." Ray argued that "This work of furnishing ministers with churches and churches with pastors is not part of the duty of a corresponding secretary." W. M. Anderson wrote a reply that was published in the *Word & Way* calling Ray's response a "gross misinterpretation." He also noted that Ray's attack on the board was not his "maiden effort" at such tactics. Anderson went on to address another of Ray's complaints about delays in publication of the minutes from the Oklahoma Baptist Convention's meeting following Smith's death. Anderson argued that circumstances following that event were "perfectly plain" as the cause for the delay.[40]

In the meantime, L. W. began a search for a pastorate. That was not as likely a solution as might seem probable. There were a number of vacant pastorates but also a number of pastors out of work. An article Marks published in *Word & Way* during this time suggested part of the problem was that many ministers were unprepared for the work. He called for increased college and seminary work to prepare men for the challenges of the pastorate and prevent their becoming "disillusioned, disgruntled kickers."[41]

The other side of that coin though was the matter of compensation for ministers. The vast majority of Oklahoma congregations could not afford a full-time pastor. Marks compiled the best data illustrating this situation for his report as historical secretary to the OBSC in 1905. The data show continuing, even remarkable, growth but also document shaky financial foundation for many of the institutions. That year, Oklahoma Territory had gained 58 new churches, bringing the total to 383, with 18,483 members after 2,110 additions by baptisms and 2,512 from other means, or slightly less than fifty per congregation. However, there were still only 136 churches with their own meeting houses and only nineteen with parsonages after an increase of eight in the prior year. Of the total churches, 269 held preaching one-fourth time, 68 one-half time, and only 46 full-time. As grim as these statistics were, the churches' plight was even worse than it might seem as even the larger congregations often required subsidies to even approach their budget needs with no more than half self-supporting. And, the progression from the subsidies provided by the Home Mission Society and Home Mission Board was both slow and uncertain. For 1903 for instance, only the church at Mangum was self-supporting with Tonkawa and Weatherford on record as attempting to reach the mark of self-sufficiency.[42]

Fortunately, one of the stronger churches within this assortment needed a pastor, especially one with Marks' qualities. Moreover, its location in Edmond, immediately adjacent to Oklahoma City, and the location of a Normal School there offered other important advantages. Upon recommendation of W. M. Anderson, Marks agreed to supply there the first Sunday in May 1904. Apparently, the deacons or some other responsible group there had requested Anderson's assistance in their search. The church then asked Marks to continue through the rest of the month and extended a formal call to him on June 3 with a salary of $100 monthly. Marks accepted and began work in the area immediately.[43]

Edmond had been established at the site of a Santa Fe railroad station in 1887 but had not drawn the number of settlers who focused on Guthrie, Kingfisher, and Oklahoma City during the land run of 1889. Within months, however, two noted town promoters located there. The first of these was Milton Reynolds who had been one of the leading boomers calling for the land opening. Reynolds first established a newspaper at Guthrie, but competitive pressure caused him to move his operations to Edmond in July where he published the first issue of the *Sun* on July 18. A few months later, Anton

Classen, who had also settled initially at Guthrie, moved to Edmond. Classen would later play a principal role in the development of Oklahoma City, but for the next few years, he and Reynolds provided the nucleus for a core of Edmond boosters who had established both the first public school house and the first church in Oklahoma Territory. Sidewalks, a tree-lined boulevard, and other improvements also set the town apart from most within a few years of settlement.

The location of the Territorial Normal School at Edmond came after community leaders quickly responded to an act of the first territorial legislature in 1890. The first classes for the Normal School were held in November 1891 in rooms offered by the Methodist Episcopal Church. These were the first higher education classes held in the new territory preceding those at the A & M at Stillwater by a month and the university at Norman by almost one year. The first Normal School building was ready for classes by January 1893.

Marks undoubtedly appreciated Edmond's progressive spirit, but the situation he faced at the Baptist church there was less encouraging. Edmond's Baptists had established the fourth church in the community in May 1890, following earlier successes by Catholics, Methodists, and Presbyterians. They completed their first building in 1894. Ten years later when Marks became pastor, the church still struggled financially. Although relatively stronger than most churches in the territory, it still required subsidies from Northern and Southern Baptist mission agencies and regularly struggled to pay the pastor's salary and other expenses.[44]

Unfortunately, financial woes were actually the least of the church's worries in spring 1904. By that time, problems in the fellowship had grown so severe that there were concerns that the church might not survive. In January, the church had voted to ask R. C. Opie, the pastor, to resign after he had responded to an earlier dispute by holding services with about twenty members at locations other than the church property. The dispute ultimately threatened the dissolution of the church. Marks commented on that potential fate in a *Word & Way* editorial describing a good meeting house and the "pretty little city" and asserted that the potential of the Normal School requires that "Baptists maintain their cause at points like this at any cost."[45]

The causes of the dispute between the pastor and the church were never defined. Opie had been involved in an Arizona land promotion deal, but that may have had no connection to the dispute. Although there were some charges of unsound doctrine, his supporters argued otherwise, and an independent committee did not comment on that charge. The committee formed from three leaders in the association after a request from the church in February. Members from each of the opposing sides from the congregation had agreed to the committee, and the church voted to accept its recommendations. W. M. Anderson from First Baptist Church, Oklahoma City, W. T. Moore from Geary, and a Mr. Green from an unidentified church in Oklahoma City formed the committee with Anderson as chair.[46]

The committee report concluded that both factions had erred, the church in seeking Opie's resignation and he and his followers' actions holding services elsewhere. It recommended that Opie resign and the church retain him and Mrs. Opie as members until they had found another church; that both should "forgive each other and band themselves together for the building up of the cause of Christ and the church"; and, that the recommendations be published in the *Baptist Flag*, *Word & Way*, and Edmond newspapers.

Unfortunately, the recommendations were not followed completely. The church approved a motion to thank the council for their advice and assistance and seemed willing to follow the recommendations, but pastor Opie denounced the work of the council. Two weeks later, a church business meeting charged Opie and his followers with maintaining separate church services and Sunday schools and publishing false reports in town newspapers. The church then passed resolutions excluding Reverend and Mrs. Opie from membership and called for revocation of his credentials. A resolution the next month declared about twenty members of the Opie faction out of fellowship with the church and offered them one month to return. There is no evidence that any took the offer of the church. Opie was shown as pastor at Hopewell by the *Edmond Sun* in March, but he also preached regularly at varied locations from the Methodist and Lutheran churches to the Pickett schoolhouse during the next few months before gaining a position as representative for an unidentified childrens' home at Guthrie.[47]

Once Marks became pastor, he called for creation of a committee to work for restoration of the members who had not returned. That action apparently helped to improve the overall fellowship of the church but does not seem to have produced a restoration of all of the disgruntled members. Nevertheless, the church soon settled into relative peace under Marks' leadership, although it regularly fell short of its financial goals. L. W. did not seem especially concerned about this matter in the first year, seeming to accept that situation while he focused on strengthening the membership in other areas.

His salary was subsidized in the amount of $600.00 with combined contributions of the Home Mission Society, the Home Mission Board, and the OBSC. He also continued to earn small amounts from book sales and newspaper subscriptions, revivals, and other efforts. Despite the subsidies, the church ended the year $34.23 short of its commitment to him for the seven months he had served. He had, however, obtained the church's agreement to adopt the calendar plan to raise his salary for subsequent years which he hoped would lead to improved giving patterns.

In the meantime, Reverend Opie's actions continued to irritate the congregation. He and his wife joined nearby Hopewell church, apparently claiming good standing with the Edmond church. Marks then requested that the association not seat the Hopewell church. The association responded as he requested but reversed that action once it was established that the church had not known of Opie's dispute with the Edmond congregation. This issue and the surrounding confusion probably account for the creation of a special committee of the OBSC to prepare a proper form of church letter to be used by churches in the territory. Marks was one of three together with Secretary C. W. Brewer who created the form.[48]

Marks continued doing some business and reporting for the *Word & Way* after assuming the pastorate at Edmond, but the newspaper's attention to Oklahoma continued to decline. His original announcement in *Word & Way* stated he would cut travel some but continue remarks and editing. However, the *Word & Way* did not print his column after the spring of 1904, although he did have some other items published during the next few months. These included reports on two different teaching institutes offered to Oklahoma and Kansas Baptists that Marks participated in.

The first was held at Edmond with Marks presiding. It apparently met at the Normal School, but there are no other details about the effort, although it probably duplicated some of the goals and content from the prior year's institute at Blackwell. That institute then moved to Winfield, Kansas for a ten-day joint effort with Baptists in that state in July. As before, it brought in numerous seminary and other resources. Marks did not seem to be on the faculty in July, probably because of pastoral and other responsibilities.[49]

In contrast, the work at Edmond freed him to do more work with the Central Association and assume new responsibilities with the OBSC. The 1904 meeting of that body asked L. W. to compile a brief biography of L. L. Smith and named him Historical Secretary. "Someone must write the story of his life and work while the facts are fresh in the memory of the people, that the record, as well as the splendid work done, may be left to the generations following." Marks' personal thoughts on that request are not available as his diary for 1904 is missing. However, his introduction to the resultant work probably captures most of his feelings. He indicated a keen awareness of his lack of ability and training as a historian, claiming only the commitment to do the "best he could under the circumstances." At the same time, L. W. was a capable writer who had a sense of history and its importance and he recognized the value of both oral reports and written records. Unfortunately, Smith's widow moved to California, and Smith's own lack of attention to historical records limited available resources greatly.[50]

The resultant *L. L. Smith of Oklahoma: A Man of God on the Frontier* consisted of ninety-five pages that better fit the definition of a festschrift, or as L.W. phrased it, a memorial, rather than a biography. Marks' biographical sketch fills sixty-nine of the ninety-five pages with the remainder consisting of "appreciations" written by eleven colleagues and friends sharing their recollections of Smith and his work from his college days through his years as secretary of the Oklahoma Baptist Convention.[51]

L.W. began compiling materials and writing Smith's colleagues and co-workers within days of the convention request. He followed that step with a number of interviews, and then began "vigorous" work on the book, drafting his first two chapters in early March. Interestingly, he began reading a history of Sherman's march to the sea the day he began writing his book. By the middle of April, he reported that he had a "good lot" of the book ready for type setting. He let the contract for printing in May and completed proofs by the end of the month.[52]

Despite his own protestations and the acknowledged limits of the book, it provided a valuable resource for understanding of Baptist work in Oklahoma Territory. Marks was prone to stress the devotional application of Smith's life and work, but he also had a critical eye for detail. Even more important, he had a sense for interpretation that made him more than a mere reporter and chronicler. Moreover, the Smith biography was only the first of many steps he would take toward earning his acknowledgment as the "stackpole" of Oklahoma historians. Besides completing the biography, Marks had also gathered a complete file of the minutes of the Oklahoma Baptist State Convention and others from the two territories along with available associational records. His 1905 report also included statistics regarding the status of work by churches in the Oklahoma Baptist

Convention. More contributions would be forthcoming in subsequent years.[53]

By this time, Marks was well established in a good church by the standards of Oklahoma Territory and had gained wide recognition for his ability and contributions. In February 1905, he formally declined further work representing the *Word & Way* until a better financial arrangement was made. He had abandoned his dream of establishing that paper in Oklahoma but only temporarily. And, even as he began a new pastorate, he was building a legacy as a historian. He still needed to supplement his income so was regularly involved in related efforts from plating spoons to raising livestock but would define 1905 as the best year yet of his ministry.

---

1. U. S. Census Reports 12th Census, Volume I (Washington D. C.: Government Printing Office, 1901) 694.

2. Marks' diaries, January 3 and 18 and January 1-18, 1903, passim; *Word & Way*, January 22, 1903.

3. Marks' diaries, February 2 and 3, 1903 and January 18 February 9, 1903, passim.

4. Marks' diaries, February 11 and 12, 1903.

5. Marks' diaries, February 13 – March 28, 1903, passim.

6. Alvin O. Turner, "Religious Traditions and Influences" in Charles Robert Goins and Danney Gobel, *Historical Atlas of Oklahoma* (Norman, OK: U of Oklahoma Press, 2006) 224-225.

7. Ibid; Alvin O. Turner, "Out of the Past," *The Oklahoma Baptist Chronicle*, Autumn, 198, 3; Compendium of the 11th Census, Part II (Government Printing Office, 1894) 265-285.

8. Ibid

9. "Marks' Remarks" in *Word & Way* October 8, 1903, June 16 and October 6, 1904(hereinafter cited as Marks Remarks.)

10. "Religious Traditions and Influences" 224-225.

11. Marks' diaries, March 29-April 6, 1903, passim.

12. *Word & Way,* 1, Marks' Remarks, April 2, 1903.

13. Ibid., Marks' Remarks October 1, 1903

14. Marks' diaries, April 3 to July 13 passim and August 1, 1903; this may have been the paper that S. M. Brown indicated *Word & Way* had purchased from a "Brother Gresham," *Word & Way,* Jan 4, 1912; There is not a complete history of Baptist newspaper work in Oklahoma and neither the varied historical studies of J.M. Gaskin nor Robert Ross mention either the *Indian Territory Baptist* or any newspaper man or other denominational figure by the name of Gresham.

15. Marks' diaries, October 10, 1903.

16. Marks' diaries, May 24, September 20, and December 20, 1903.

17. Marks' diaries, November 4, 1903.

18. Marks' diaries, September 17 and October 24 190 ; Marks' Remarks, November 5, 12, 19, 1903.

19. Marks' Remarks, July 2, 9, and 30, 1903; Oklahoma Baptist State Convention Reports, 1903.

20. Marks' Remarks, August 27 and September 3, 1903.

21. Marks' diaries, November 7, 1903; Marks' Remarks, November 5, 12, and 19, 1903.

22. OBSC Reports 1903; Marks' Remarks, October 8, 1903; Marks' diaries, November 17-19, 1903; Reports Central Baptist Association, 1902 and 1903.

23. Bob Blackburn and Alvin O. Turner, *The First Family* (Oklahoma City, OK: First Baptist Church, 1990) 72; Marks' diaries, July 9, 1903.

24. J. R. Gaskin, *Baptist Milestones in Oklahoma* (Good Printing Co., 1966) 125-131; Marks' diaries, May 31, 1903; Marks' Remarks, July 30, August 6, and October 29, 1903; The First Family 22; J. M. Gaskin to L. W. Marks II, August 6, 1977, Marks family files.

25. *The Southern Baptist Convention*, 183-186.

26. Marks' Remarks, December 17, 1903 and January 14, 1904; Phyllis W. Sapp, *Lighthouse on the Corner* , Century Press 1964) 18.

27. Marks' diaries, June 6, 11, and July 7-15, 1903, passim; Marks' Remarks, July 23, 1903.

28. *Baptist Milestones in Oklahoma*, 49-51; T. R. Corr, "A Brief History of the Oklahoma State Baptist College, Blackwell, Oklahoma," *The Chronicles of Oklahoma*, Vol. 20, No. 4, 396-397.

29. Gaskin. Milestones 49; Marks' Remarks, October 8, 1903.

30. Marks' Remarks, July 3 and October 8 1903; L. L. Smith report to the Central Baptist Association, August, 1903.

31. Marks' Diaries April 6 and 13, 1903.

32 .Ibid; L. L. Smith report to the Central District Baptist Association, August 11-13, 1903.

33. Reports, Central Baptist Association, 1904.

34. *Baptist Milestones in Oklahoma* 146-147; Smith report, August 1903; Marks' diaries, November 11 and 22, 1903; Marks' Remarks, October 15 and December 17, 1903; *Word & Way*, November 26, 1903.

35. Reports, Central District Baptist Association for 1901 and 1902.

36. Marks' diaries, April 21, June 8 and 24, and July 24, 1903.

37. Marks' diaries, October 13, 1903.

38. Marks' diaries, October 22 and end pages of 1903.

39. Marks' Remarks, March 3, 1904.

40. Marks Remarks, December 17, 1903.

41. Marks Remarks April 21, 1904

42. Marks' Remarks, April 21, 1904; OBSC Convention reports, 1903-1905, passim.

43. Marks' Remarks, May 26 and June 9, 1904; Minutes, First Baptist Church (FBC) Edmond, Oklahoma, June 3 and 12, 1904.

44. Stan Hoig, Edmond: *The First Century* (Edmond Historic Preservation Trust, 1987) 7; Stan Hoig, *The Early Years of Edmond* (Hoig, 1976) 6-9, 11, 18-19, and 23.

45. FBC Minutes, January 7, 1904; Marks' Remarks, May 26, 1904.

46. FBC Edmond Minutes, February 4, 18, and 19, 1904.

47. *Edmond Sun*, March 23, May 11, June 8 and 15, 1904.

48. Central Association Reports, August 16-18, 1904; OBSC Reports, 1904.

49. Marks' Remarks, June 2 and 9, 1904.

50. Marks' Remarks, June 2 and 9, 1904; L. W. Marks, L. L. Smith of Oklahoma (Times Journal Publishing Co., 1905) 3-5.

51. Ibid.

52. Marks' diaries February 15-16, March 7-8, April 4 and 17-24 and May 22 and 31 1905.

53. OBSC Reports, 1905.

1917
— First Baptist Church Edmond — in snow —

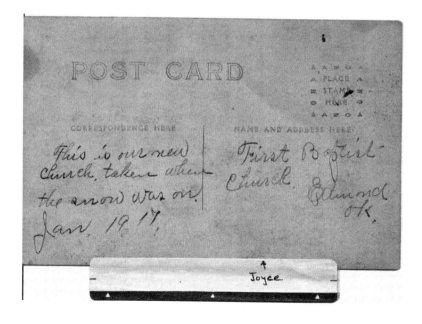

POST CARD

PLACE
STAMP
HERE

CORRESPONDENCE HERE

NAME AND ADDRESS HERE

This is our new Church, taken when the snow was on. Jan. 1917,

First Baptist Church. Edmond Ok.

Joyce

YOU ARE WELCOME AT

Come Thou With Us and We Will Do Thee Good—N; m. 10:29.

Thy Gates Shall Be Open Continually—Isa. 60:11

THE FIRST BAPTIST CHURCH,

Edmond, Oklahoma.

L. W. MARKS, Th. M., Pastor

JULY.							OCTOEER						
S	M	T	W	T	F	S	S	M	T	W	T	F	S
.	.	.	.	.	1	2	.	.	.	.	.	.	1
3	4	5	6	7	8	9	2	3	4	5	6	7	8
10	11	12	13	16	15	16	9	1	11	12	13	14	15
17	18	19	20	21	22	23	16	17	18	19	20	21	22
24	25	26	27	28	29	30	23	24	25	26	27	28	29
31	.						30	31					

AUGUST							NOVEMBER						
.	.	1	2	3	4	5	6	.	.	1	2	3	4	5
7	8	9	10	11	12	13	6	7	8	9	10	11	12
14	15	16	17	18	19	20	13	14	15	16	17	18	19
21	22	23	24	25	26	27	20	21	22	23	24	25	26
28	29	30					27	28	29	30			

SEPTEMBER.							DECEMBER						
.	.	.	.	1	2	3	.	.	.	.	1	2	3
4	5	6	7	8	9	10	4	5	6	7	8	9	10
11	12	13	14	15	16	17	11	12	13	14	15	16	17
18	19	2	21	22	23	24	18	19	20	21	22	23	24
25	26	27	28	29	30	.	25	26	27	28	29	30	.

SERVICE CALENDER.

Preaching Every Sunday at 11 a. m., and 8 p. m.

Prayer Meeting Every Thursday at 8 p. m.

Sunday School Every Sunday at 10 a. m. T. N. Horner, Supt.

B. Y. P. U. Every Sunday at 7 p. m. Eva Carmichael. Pres.

Teachers Meeting Every Friday at 8 p. m. Pastor, Leader.

venant and Business Meeting, The First Thursday in Each Month at 8. p. m.

City Hall
Edmond, OK

"Pop" Marks Mayor 1912-13

over

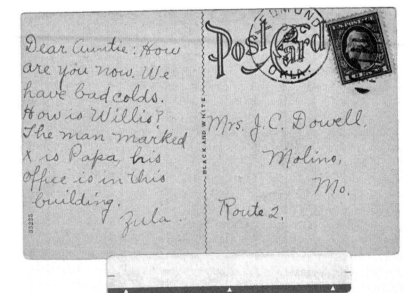

Dear Auntie: How
are you now. We
have bad colds.
How is Willis?
The man marked
X is Papa, his
office is in this
building.
            Zula.

Post Card

Mrs. J.C. Dowell.
      Molino,
          Mo.
   Route 2.

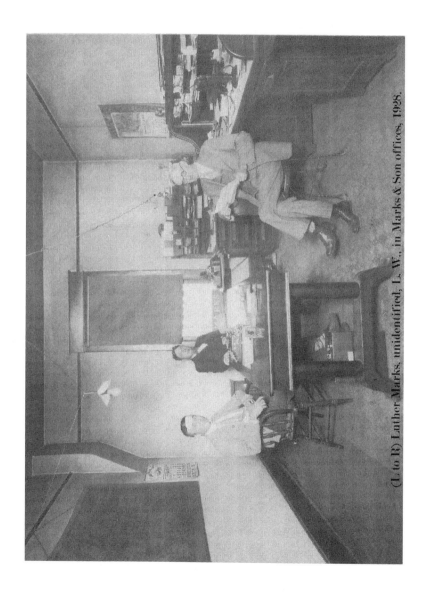

(L to R) Luther Marks, unidentified, L. W., in Marks & Son offices, 1928.

L. W. & Sadie (Pop & Mamoo) ca. 1935

Pastorates in Edmond, OK And Lamar, MO

L. W. seemed to enjoy every task he undertook from selling subscriptions to plating spoons, and he was always willing to accept a level of sacrifice to promote his progressive goals. The measure of that commitment was seen in his expressions of regret any time his work took him away from his family. In contrast, he was most likely to express deep satisfaction during times with his wife and children and in the early stages of work in a new ministry. The beginning of his work at Edmond, the completion of the Smith biography, and his work in the Central Association explain his satisfaction at the end of 1905 when he would report he had never had so much for which to be thankful.

The work of restoring all of the members lost in the dispute with pastor Opie continued throughout that year without complete resolution, but he had gained progress on that front and others. He celebrated more than 134 in attendance at Sunday school in February and the church's improved mission offerings the next month. He also saw prospects for the church as very encouraging. He led the members in conducting a religious census of the community, an unusual practice at the time, and was delighted to find "scores of Baptists" he had never heard of.[1]

The improved spirit of the church was celebrated seen in a big picnic and chicken fry his first summer there. The chicken was fried in a giant kettle of lard, and families brought other food for a dinner on the grounds at a nearby body of water. That offered the opportunity for swimming as well as baptizing after a day of eating, singing, and preaching. Marks gleefully reported that "everybody was delighted," and he was undoubtedly among the most pleased by the event. A revival the next month and other efforts during the year led to at least twenty new memberships from conversions and other means.[2]

Even church finances gave a basis for celebration even though the church lagged on its payments to Marks through the first nine months of the year, peaking at an accumulated shortfall of $32.82 in June. By October, however, his salary was current, and the church had adopted a new budget. He was pleased by the church's adoption of the Southern Baptist Convention Sunday School Board plan of study at the same time. Even more exciting, plans were proceeding toward the purchase of a parsonage. Both of these developments meant even more than they might have at another time as Marks was encountering continuing problems with the home he had purchased two years before in Oklahoma City.[3]

He had elected to rent the house rather than sell it upon his move to Edmond, but his tenant began to fall behind by June and owed more than $72.00 in rent by October. Marks was sympathetic to the family's financial plight but was unable to subsidize them while still making a house payment and paying rent in Edmond. The tenant also seemed unwilling to discuss a resolution of the matter, so L. W. proceeded reluctantly with a lawsuit, assuring his diary that "everybody says I did right." He then found that the property had been damaged by the tenant. He finally sold the property for a price that included the deed to two lots in Edmond the next spring.

He was most pleased by the results and typically soon planted one of the recently acquired lots in cotton.[4]

Other developments added to his satisfaction. His biography of L. L. Smith was well received by the convention, and he continued to enjoy opportunities for wider service. He attended association meetings at varied locations in the two territories where he continued to solicit funds for the orphanage and other causes, but most of his efforts involved the Baptist Young People's Union (BYPU), a growing territorial temperance movement, and Oklahoma Baptist College.

L. W. worked as a representative for the BYPU promoting its spread among the churches at association meetings. He occasionally received limited compensation from the convention for these efforts, but most of his work was based on his commitment to education in its broadest sense and to a growing interest in young people. His growing attention to the BYPU seems to have corresponded with the maturation of his own children. He promoted Sunday school for similar reasons and presided at a three-day associational Sunday school convention hosted by the church at Edmond in 1905.

The community appreciated the new pastor as well, and he quickly became a regular speaker for varied lodges and other groups. A speech he delivered in May 1905 to the Edmond post of the Grand Army of the Republic is especially interesting as an example of his thinking about war and especially the Civil War that had affected his life so drastically. He began with reference to Ephesians 6:11 connecting the idea of the whole armor of God with the "strange phenomenon" of the soldier. He noted that the world honored soldiers for fighting and killing and that God had also honored many soldiers who were among his best servants. L. W. then asserted that the success of armies is always in direct proportion to the Christian influence within the camps; correspondingly, that quality had also shaped the years after the war. The world had seen nothing equal to the fierceness and destruction of the Civil War. It also witnessed General U. S. Grant's magnanimous treatment of the vanquished Confederate forces. And, the world "never saw a nobler sight than the shattered ranks" of those who returned to rebuild their ruined homes and lands.[1]

He echoed similar themes in an undated message entitled, "A Day of Memories." He began by contrasting youth's preoccupation with "air castles to be" and the evening of life where one lives on memories. He went on to celebrate the history of the United States which had created a nation that became an asylum for the oppressed. For Marks, the American mission to the world had been made possible by the heroes from its wars. He then focused on the Civil War, asserting that although the reasons for its carnage had never been adequately justified, it had produced heroes from both sides. The nation should remember their sacrifices as well as those of the women who lost husbands and sons but experienced neither "touch of comrade or shout of victory." He concluded with the assertion that "The war is over. Every true soldier is glad."[6]

Both of these messages contain content and themes typical of the era but not necessarily what could be expected of a Southerner and son of a slain Confederate soldier. L. W.'s comments reveal a much more forgiving spirit than was often the case among those who shared his experience. The talks are also remarkable for his apparent disregard for the Southern "Lost Cause" movement. Further, they reveal a man who was willing to grapple with deep issues such as those inherent in an effort to reconcile the horrors of war with the Christian message.

Marks' successes in community and church added to his growing reputation within the state. As a result, he was given serious consideration for two salaried positions with the convention at the 1905 meeting, first as corresponding secretary and then as Sunday school secretary. C. W. Brewer continued as corresponding secretary, and W. A. Moorer gained the newly created Sunday school position. Marks indicated no disappointment about these decisions and seemed to concur with both selections. He respected Brewer's work and had been able to work closely with him and Moorer was one of his close friends. L. W. was also content in the Edmond church and as historical secretary. However, the historical office was not compensated, and he was not always reimbursed for his expenses acquiring material or for other duties. For instance, the Board voted to compensate him in the amount of $50.00 for his compilation of minutes from varied associational and other territorial organizations but did not have the money to actually pay him.[7]

As seen in his efforts at Wyaconda, Marks had been a long-term supporter of temperance but he reported no work on behalf of that movement in Oklahoma until 1905. His renewed interest at that time was probably linked to developments in Oklahoma territorial politics and his work as a pastor. The U. S. government had long prohibited the liquor traffic in Indian Territory, but there were no such restrictions on the Oklahoma side where liquor laws were at best "loose." By 1904, however, sentiment favoring restraints on trade in alcoholic beverages, if not an absolute ban, was growing in force. The Women's Christian Temperance Union had been organized in both territories since 1900, but the growth of the Anti-Saloon League four years later added new zest to the movement in the emerging state.[8]

The first chapters for the League organized at McAlester in 1904, and other local clubs soon followed. In turn, dozens of Oklahoma Territory communities then began to petition to make their towns dry. Their efforts were expedited by favorable court rulings that held that an applicant for a saloon license had to obtain thirty signatures within the ward where the saloon was to be established. That requirement was then applied retroactively. By the end of 1905, newspaper men were estimating from forty to one-hundred towns were dry that previously had saloons. L. W. participated in varied campaigns in the territory promoting temperance at associational meetings and in special locations at sites as far removed from Edmond as Elk City. The campaign in Edmond peaked in 1905-06 with Marks, A. M. Virden of the Methodists, and other church leaders calling to dry up Edmond. Marks was always inclined to interdenominational cooperation, but by this time, the issue transcended some personal differences as well. L. W. had confronted Virden some time previously about the latter's efforts to persuade some of the choir members from the Baptist Church to join with the Methodists.[9]

Marks captured many elements of the prohibitionists' expectations and his particular hope for Oklahoma in a song he wrote about this time while at Edmond.

> *The Land of Beautiful Homes*
> We've homes in beautiful south-west
> That land more fair than all the rest.
> Its plains are rich, its valleys fair,
> And happy homes are building there.

CHORUS:
Oh, land so fair, can there yet be,
Still homes from sin that I may free?
May free, may free, from sin may free,
Our happy homes from sin may free.

The tempters come with deadly snare,
To capture hearts of young and fair.
And rum has come with deadly blight,
To lure our sons from paths of right.
(CHORUS)

Its rivers flow, its springs abound,
And fairest fruits can there be found;
But sin abounds (has come) with deadly snare,
To ruin the homes now (that are) building there.
(CHORUS)

There is a cure for all its woe,
Come tell it out that all may know.
If men will come to Calvary's tree,
The Saviour's blood is flowing free.
(CHORUS)

Oh, who will come and bear away,
The cross that JESUS bore one day.
And go through all this land so fair,
And save the homes now building here.
(CHORUS)

And when we've gone through all the land,
And told to every sin-cursed man,

We'll meet some day in realms more fair;

The Saviour's building homes up there.

(CHORUS)[10]

The Edmond campaign began with a meeting possibly held at the First Baptist church the evening of February 19. Event speakers included a Church of Christ preacher and the head of the Anti-Saloon League whose talk Marks rated as "long and dry." Later that spring, Carrie Nation, the noted temperance promoter who then resided at Guthrie, spoke in Edmond. However, the prohibitionist forces were unsuccessful though their campaign continued into the next year with at least two other meetings. Both L. W. and Virden spoke at the May meeting held at the Methodist Church with Virden cutting some "high capers" according to Marks. In early July, another meeting about the "saloon fight" was held at the Normal School but by this time, the struggle had been redefined. On June 19, 1906, Congress passed an omnibus bill providing for the organization of the new state; thereafter the dry forces focused on the forthcoming Constitution of the State of Oklahoma.[11]

Oklahoma's Baptists and their religious and other reform-oriented allies would win this campaign and achieve statewide prohibition. The Enabling Act required a continuation of restraints on sale of alcoholic beverages in Indian Territory for twenty-one years. Petitions bearing almost 5,000 signatures calling for similar provisions statewide greeted the Constitutional delegates who gathered at Guthrie in November 1906. The force of the petitions was buttressed further when the Anti-Saloon League sent its top lobbyist from Washington, D. C. to lead the dry forces at the convention. In reality, however, the result was a foregone conclusion for two reasons. Charles Haskell, who would be the state's first governor, was one of the most influential men at the convention, and he favored statewide prohibition. He persuaded the convention's president, William H. Murray, to appoint a sympathetic committee to address the liquor question.[12]

Political machinations aside, Haskell's position and the votes of the delegates were shaped both by their own convictions and their recognition of the voters' beliefs. Dry forces were in the ascendancy and their lobbyists filled the halls at the meetings of the convention. C. W. Brewer from the OBSC was among the most prominent and influential lobbyists. Marks had made the motion from the OBSC temperance committee, creating that responsibility for Brewer.[13]

That action undoubtedly represented a high water mark for Marks' contribution toward statewide prohibition, but he made no reference to it in his diaries celebrating instead a bigger achievement from the 1906 convention. As recording secretary, he took many of the minutes for the OBSC when the convention passed a resolution calling for unification with their Indian Territory counterparts. The two conventions had taken steps toward the unification on a number of occasions after 1900, but territorial rivalries and other issues prevented their success. In 1905, the OBSC passed a resolution calling for unification, but it was rejected by the Indian Territory Convention. Once statehood was on the horizon, however, the climate changed dramatically.

On November 9, 1906, the Baptist General Convention of Indian Territory met for its annual meeting at the First Baptist Church of Shawnee, while the Oklahoma Baptist State Convention gathered at the nearby Methodist Church. Upon votes of the respective delegates, the two conventions adjourned *sine die* and gathered in front of the Methodist church before marching arm in arm from there to the nearby opera house where they formed the Baptist General Convention of Oklahoma (BGCO). The delegates were called to order by M. E. Early and sang "Blest Be the Tie that Binds." The first prayer was offered by J. S. Murrow, the senior statesman among Baptist missionaries in Oklahoma. J. A. Scott then presided over the rest of the meeting.[14]

The BGCO retained the principle of dual alignment with the respective mission boards of the Southern and Northern Baptist Conventions. Marks also obtained establishment of a historical society to "preserve the memories of the heroes of the cross" in Oklahoma. The convention then named him historical secretary as he had been for the Oklahoma Territory organization. Theses and other accomplishments reflected the general spirit of cooperation and harmony attending the merger. The exception to that rule came arose over differences between Indian and Oklahoma Territory delegates over how many, if any, Home Mission Society and Home Mission Board employees could serve on the boards of the BGCO. The convention decision to excluded employees of outside mission societies from the BGCO executive board stirred some hard feelings but not enough to dampen the sprit of celebration.

In contrast, Marks, expressed some concerns about another matter that arose during the meeting. Ironically, that problem stemmed from a development he had played a key role in the previous July. At that time, the Oklahoma and Indian Territory BYPU had united and held their first encampment at Sulphur. Marks regarded both of those achievements as a "gratifying success." He was less enthusiastic about related proposals that then came from the Sulphur community that seemed to represent an attack on Oklahoma Baptist College. Evidently, one speaker had suggested the possibility of creating a Baptist college there in conjunction with the encampment. L. W. attempted to "meet with the enemies of our school" at the time but without success. An offer of "four blocks" for encampment purposes by a representative from Sulphur to the convention then added to his concern. Sulphur's offer soon fell by the wayside as did annual encampments in the area until the beginnings of Falls Creek Baptist Assembly a decade later, a few miles west of Sulphur.[15]

Marks' concerns about the college had increased greatly in the preceding two years. He had begun service as a trustee in 1904 along with his regular fund-raising efforts at associational and other meetings. He was then named as one of three trustees for the institution by the 1906 convention. In fact, Marks frequently served as a de facto business manager during much of the preceding two years due to financial pressures and related administrative flux at the college. The college's first president had resigned in June 1903, and E. D. Cave, a faculty member, was made acting president. The financial agent was dismissed and replaced a month later by A. P. Stone who added presidential duties later that year. At the close of the academic year in spring 1904, the college's debt stood at $22,000, showing no progress from the convention efforts of the previous year.[16]

The financial problems were compounded by faculty concerns arising from dismissal of one teacher in spring 1905 who had not met board expectations. The tensions inherent in such matters grew even more when one of the trustees discussed the issue and other board matters with friends and faculty. An April meeting of the board was intended primarily to hire faculty members, settle new contracts, and similar matters but was prolonged by wrangling between two board members and President

Stone. Marks sided with Stone and "decided to clear the air" apparently with some success.[17]

He and Stone then spent a day in council during their attendance at the Southern Baptist Convention held in Kansas City, Missouri that year. Two weeks later, the two met again in an "emergency meeting" with Stone in "a peck of trouble" after a new round of rumors began floating about the college. Marks then prepared the catalogue for the next year's offerings. He met with Stone again in conjunction with graduation exercises in June, indicating the president was disturbed and "a little petulant" about continuing problems at the college. While most students continued to be pleased with their educational experience there, a few had been upset by publicity surrounding the wrangling over the faculty member's dismissal. He had added to the quarrel by continuing to publicize his issues with his treatment by the college.

A state of crisis continued during subsequent months. Stone agreed to waive his salary for July in response to cash flow concerns while Marks sent out letters to supporters trying to raise the needed funds. At the October board meeting, L. W., Stone, and J. W. McAtee, chairman of the faculty, met with another board member regarding a misunderstanding with a faculty member. L. W. then drew up new faculty contracts. The lack of substantive progress and continuing irritants from other matters finally led to Stone's resignation at the January 1906 board meeting. Otherwise, harmony prevailed among board members who then concurred on appointment of J. W. McAtee as acting president.[18]

Despite the board's consensus, the situation deteriorated even further in the next few months virtually hamstringing Marks' ongoing efforts at fund-raising. In

April, the board dismissed three faculty members and approved hiring of their replacements. However, the board was unable to agree on a replacement for Stone. E. D. Cameron finally won out over the candidacy of A. E. Booth in June. Cameron then came to Blackwell only to spend a week before deciding not to take the position. Marks then wired an offer to Booth, but he declined. The board declared the position open in July.[19]

Marks referred to yet more "knotty problems" at that meeting besides the president's replacement. The board was unable to fill all faculty positions, leaving Marks to complete the year's catalogue and to search with H. A. Porter and another board member for a president and music teacher. Despite these difficulties, the school gained its best enrollment ever that fall. The September board meeting celebrated that achievement and offered Marks the position as financial manager. The faculty also supported his selection, but he agreed to do so only on a temporary basis. He reported an offer of $100 per month, but the financial stance of the college had not changed, and he knew he could not be assured of regular pay. At the same time, his decision also reflected his commitment to a pastoral ministry even though he had resigned the pastorate at Edmond two months earlier.[20]

Something dramatic had clearly affected the situation at the Edmond church, but what that might have been cannot be defined. His community activities continued to be well received and personally satisfying. He was especially pleased to be chosen to award public school diplomas in May. That situation changed in June although his diaries gave no prior indication of any significant disruptions in the harmony that had prevailed at the end of 1905. There had been problems with two deacons from the beginning of his service at Edmond, but he had confronted both during his first months at the church and the problems seemed to settle down thereafter. Marks would report subsequent differences, but both supported him on a number of initiatives, and one had sent the Marks' family a chicken when he was ill. Marks reciprocated, using *Word & Way* publicity and letters to try and solicit funds to help one of the men with expenses for eye surgery.[21]

The only other time Marks used *Word & Way* for such purposes also occurred in the spring 1906 when he solicited help for the costs of a parsonage at Edmond. There had been some problems with the church's fulfillment of that commitment, and the whole endeavor seemed at risk in January when the church began considering abandonment of the project. A motion to that effect failed in early January, and a new committee for the parsonage was appointment at the end of that month. In March, that body reported they had closed a deal for a house on three lots. The church approved that deal along with a provision that the Marks family should pay "reasonable rent" until the property was paid for. The Marks family moved into the new "pastorium" in May. Although L. W. regarded the coming and going of church members who wanted to inspect the property as a "considerable bother," he regarded the acquisition as a major achievement for the church. Nevertheless, it also contributed to a growing financial crisis at the church.[22]

Marks' diaries do not give much attention to financial problems at the church, but it had experienced frequent shortfalls meeting his salary during 1905. And, even as the congregation planned a parsonage, the deficit grew to a high of $85.71 in March 1906. Oddly, the members voted to forego a $200.00 annual subsidy from the Home Mission Society during the April business meeting.

Financial woes and related dissent grew in succeeding months.

That spring, Marks began pushing for a tent revival on the church grounds. The meeting lasted from June 14-25 and was most successful with standing room only and some people turned away at least one evening. The church, however, had to advance the funds for the tabernacle materials, and that added to the perception of financial pressure. Marks did most of the work constructing the frame for the tent, and the church would eventually recoup its investment in canvas and wood. Nevertheless, members seemed to feel paying for a parsonage plus revival expenses and the pastor's salary was asking too much. Marks called on the members publicly and sharply as the revival drew to a close in an effort to resolve the matter.[23]

Some of the members were offended by his criticism, but close to $40.00 of the shortfall was received. Still, the financial situation remained discouraging, and only $4.00 was received for his June salary. He reported a good feeling after services later that month, and he had sold the lumber and canvas used for the meeting, so most of that cost had been recovered. A week later, however, he met with the financial committee and offered to resign if they would agree to pay up. The church accepted his resignation as the month drew to a close. L. W. and Sadie held another of their long conversations with both reporting relief at its conclusion. Their relief was disrupted temporarily by the settlement process with L. W. reporting that the financial committee had tried hard to "figure me out" of some of the money owed but had not succeeded.[24]

In the meantime, he had received an invitation to Palisade, Colorado in view of a call to a church there.

Then, as now, the area was known for its peach production, and he was pleased to find "everybody (was) rich and making money by the hatful." He preached at that church and others in the area during the month, but had no other duties. That allowed him the opportunity for a vacation with mountain climbing and regional sightseeing tours including Salt Lake City where he heard an organ recital at the Mormon Tabernacle. He enjoyed all of this greatly but frequently noted how he wished for his wife and children to be able to experience it with him.

He also read a number of popular books from the era and was especially impressed by Ralph Connor's *Black Rock*. Connor was the pen name for Charles W. Gordon, a Canadian Presbyterian minister who would become Canada's leading writer in the era. *Black Rock*, as his other books, called for progressive social change consistent with the belief that "religion is the soul out of which well doing and well being spring." Marks enthused over the book and its ideas as he had *In His Steps* while at the seminary, noting he felt stronger after reading it.[25]

L. W., of course, also found numerous opportunities to work. He made visits on behalf of the Palisade church, enjoyed helping one member make peach crates, and wrote about churches in the area *Word & Way*. His preaching was well received with one member telling him his sermon had been the best he ever received, but the church had a policy that obligated them to hear a number of preachers; he never heard anything more form the church. He had also preached at the Montrose church which extended a call that he rejected because the salary was only $700.00.[26]

He then returned to Edmond and began preparation for a move to Missouri after arranging for Sadie and the children to stay with the Jenkins family temporarily. The

Sunday before he left Edmond, Marks taught a Sunday school class and heard the new pastor H. Wallace and praised the message he heard. Once the move was completed, he began a round of preaching at churches throughout the state and resumed work as a representative for *Word & Way*. *Word & Way* then offered him a good salary as circulation editor but he declined a full-time position and continued his search for a pastorate.[27]

Through October and November, at least six churches offered him a position, but none of the salaries approached the level he sought. His search ended the next month. On December 22, he preached at Lamar, Missouri where he was favorably impressed by a fine Sunday school and a good congregation. The membership reciprocated his regard and extended a unanimous call on December 28 at $900.00 a year. His first Sunday evening sermon as pastor contained "lots of noise and some good points." That also seemed an apt description of the preceding year's activities. As the year ended, he was happy to be located again, making plans for his family to join him and compiling a list of the membership; he would begin calling on the members and prospects the next day.[28]

Both the congregation and wider community responded positively to Marks' work during the next few weeks. The *Lamar Leader*, the self-proclaimed "family paper of Barton County," welcomed him, noting the reception of four new members of the church and "unusual interest" stirred by his efforts. The political, economic, cultural, and environment correspondingly seemed made to order for Marks' commitments. Lamar's prosperity was at an all time high by 1900. It had recovered from the devastation of the Civil War that had almost leveled the town after the return of agricultural prosperity and the expansion of the railroads and coal mines. Those ingredients also assured relative prosperity for the rest of the county while Lamar's status as county seat and a railroad center made it the trade center for the county and parts beyond.[29]

Lamar offered the richest range of cultural opportunities the Marks' family had ever encountered. Accordingly, Marks' diaries contain regular entries about his and Sadie's attendance, often with one of the children, at the town's opera house. The Kemp Sisters Wild West Show, China relief presentations, varied lectures, musical performances, motion pictures, and a hypnotism demonstration were representative. Marks was especially fascinated with the latter "strange phenomenon" but seemed to enjoy most such events and took the children to the movies frequently. Beyond these occasions, there were also traveling tent shows and circuses and the activities at Lamar College equaled or surpassed those the family had enjoyed in Edmond.[30]

One result of the convergence of these opportunities and the maturation of his children is seen in an increased number of entries about them. Marks enjoyed his children at every stage, but his pleasure in them seemed to increase as they aged. Their growth also permitted increased occasions for fishing at the numerous sites accessible in the Lamar area. His notes about his children also show their progress in their faith and he reported baptizing Paul and Luther in 1907. Other diary notes dealt with a birthday party for Zulah, establishing savings accounts for the children, and similar entries. Community prosperity and the good spirit that prevailed at the church during most of his time there also meant he was able to give the children more gifts at Christmas and birthday. The children gained even more with frequent gifts given by church members in conjunction with church events. L. W.

and Sadie were also treated well. He estimated the value of the pounding they received at 1907 Christmas of $18.00 plus a turkey from the Sunday school class. He received a $5.25 gift of a "fine tie" and a box of handkerchiefs while Sadie got gloves and a handkerchief, and all the children received small gifts.[32]

One marked exception to this happy pattern took place in early February with the "bloodiest crime in the city's history." The church janitor Joe Edwards and his wife were murdered by Lee Hart who evidently believed they were encouraging his wife to leave him. He first shot Mrs. Edwards while attempting to kill his own wife. The bullet intended for Mrs. Hart grazed her cheek but killed Mrs. Edwards instantly. Mr. Edwards was then wounded seriously moments later when he rushed to try and protect his wife Hart then fled the immediate area. He evaded determined efforts to capture him but his mangled body was found the next morning, an apparent suicide on the nearby railroad tracks. Marks maintained contact with Edwards for the next few weeks, reporting him somewhat better on March 10. Edwards eventually recovered, dying of old age in 1920.[32]

All of the excitement aside, the church responded to L. W.'s leadership with numerical growth and other measures of progress and he encountered no major stumbling blocks. His salary was even paid on time during most of his tenure there. He reported almost thirty professions of faith followed by baptisms in his first three months with almost one-half that many added by letter. His diary notes sometimes included reports from meetings he assisted with or held elsewhere, so all of those conversions and letters might not have been at Lamar; though, most certainly were. The impact of that growth was directly reflected in attendance figures. He exulted over 112 in attendance at Sunday school on February 3, reported the largest yet two weeks later, and then another record, 150 in mid March. The rate of growth leveled off thereafter, but regular revivals and other events kept the church growing. Marks' preaching also seems to have been reinvigorated with his diary occasionally giving some indication of his reflections. One such instance dealt with his fascination with the idea of a sermon on the face of Jesus.[33]

In that climate, Marks initiated regular weekly PM studies on Thursdays, initiated a cradle roll and home department, and introduced new songbooks to the congregation. He also encouraged the congregation to assist a new church at Sedalia. Some members opposed that action, but the church still collected $40.75 to aid yet another sister congregation. L. W. noted his pleasure with their support of missions, including funding for the continuing growth of a mission Sunday school on the east side of Lamar in the fall of 1902. Earlier that year, he had held meetings on the lawn at the school house in that area, and interest had continued thereafter. The school board rejected continuing use of the school building, so he began efforts to raise funds even as he expressed doubts about his capacity to do so. He succeeded by some undetermined fashion reporting that the mission was "doing fine" at the end of the year. By that spring, he reported fifty-two in attendance at the site and had earlier noted at least three conversions from those who attended.[34]

L. W. also preached regularly at the county poor farm and at outlying churches. And, as he had previously in both Missouri and Oklahoma, his commitments took him to area and state association meetings. He preached and took minutes for such meetings on a number of occasions and continued selling both stock and subscriptions for

Word & Way. For a time at least, he added more to his income selling subscriptions to a farm magazine. That magazine sponsored a contest with a piano as the grand prize for the person who could determine the number of dots arranged on a page of the magazine. He spent hours in fruitless pursuit of that goal but still had time for an occasional carpentry project, building a bookshelf for one woman and roofing a house and building a shed for his friend, the associational missionary and longtime friend J B. Frisbe. He supplemented his income still further with sale of milk and eggs from the chickens and cows he raised.[35]

His pursuit of extra income despite regular pay at the church illustrates the financial pressures created by his family, now numbering nine children. Yet, he turned down an offer to move to a nearby church that would have raised his salary to $1,000 yearly. The continued positive response of the Lamar church and his own relative prosperity allowed him that option. In addition, part of his desire to stay in Lamar at that time undoubtedly stemmed from his growing political involvement as the town's drys fought to establish prohibition in their community.

The years of Marks' pastorate in Lamar were at or near the peak for the progressive movement in Missouri and prohibition was the primary goal for many. The Democratic Party had held the governorship since 1873, and not all of the party establishment favored the reform efforts. In St. Louis, however, a crusading district attorney had built a ground swell of support that would result in a progressive take-over of the party and the adoption of their agenda for the state. Joseph W. "Holy Joe" Folks, won the gubernatorial election in 1904 with his "Missouri idea," emphasizing a moral dimension to the progressive agenda, calling for prohibition, Sunday closings, and other moralistic measures.[36]

A heated prohibition campaign emerged in Lamar in the fall of 1907 after three years of increasing political involvement across the state. In 1904, the state legislature had passed laws providing for pure food and drugs, railroad rate reductions and maximum freight rates, anti lobby measures, antitrust regulations, prohibition on child labor, and providing for the initiative and referendum. Those direct democracy features were then submitted to the state's voters in 1904 but rejected. Consequently, Initiative and Referendum forces launched a year-long campaign to educate the voters about the laws. This action resulted in their subsequent passage while also stimulating local political interest in direct participation in government.[37]

The next legislature then encouraged local groups to organize in support of enforcement of dram shop laws. This included recent provisions for state licensing of dram shops and Sunday closings. In October, L. W. led in formation of an anti saloon league to promote local option throughout Barton County. Marks' goal was to "knock them out in both county and town." He was elected president of the incipient organization. Dr. J. J. Martin, the pastor of the Lamar Methodist Church, was another of the prime movers and spokesmen for the organization and its efforts.[38]

The anti saloon campaign began in earnest the next month. Marks' diaries are dominated by related entries about his work for local option for the rest of the year. He spoke to at least three different groups and took a side trip to nearby Ft. Scott for preaching and to report on their enforcement of dry laws. With two parades in the first two weeks of December, regular lectures and meetings of the

Women's Christian Temperance Union, a rally at the opera house, and a massive campaign by church women, Marks grew in confidence as the election approached. On December 7, he reported "the tide has turned our way." He remained hopeful on the eve of the election five days later but expected the liquor forces to fight "to the last ditch." He reported "great rejoicing" the next day; dry forces had won the county by 250 votes and in the town by 28 votes. Marks noted "Our women were too much for them . . ."; though, the liquor forces had "bought some and fooled more."[39]

In fact, the election victory soon proved to be only the first stage of the battle to make Barton County dry. Amid concerns about resistance from defeated forces, L. W. began work with a newly formed law enforcement league; L. W. presided at the first meeting. He discussed enforcement issues in Lamar noting describing a great deal of evidence against some businesses. At the same time, he stressed the group "had no one to get even with; they didn't want to array one section of our citizenship against another . . ." He also acknowledged concerns that citizens and friends might have to choose between enforcement and protecting relationships.

Dr. J. J. Martin then addressed the group defining problems beyond enforcement of liquor laws, including regular reports of buying and selling of votes at elections. Other speakers acknowledged evidence of business compliance on the liquor issue but urged continued vigilance. The editor of the *Democrat*, which had supported the drys from the beginning, supported the league as well. He quoted Marks' goal of not working a hardship on any business or prosecution without sufficient cause. "This is a sensible course and if the league continues to follow it as we believe it will, its work will meet with the approval of all good citizens . . ."[40]

The editor's optimism about community support was not supported by developments during the next few months. In fact, dry forces soon began complaining about the lack of enforcement by local law enforcement officials. Numerous reports dotted the papers about inadequate enforcement with businesses that had been saloons previously and fraternal clubs among the most frequent violators. At times, related developments approached low comedy while still reflecting problems of enforcement. For instance, the town marshal arrested one individual who had sneaked from the back of a local pharmacy with a half gallon of whiskey. The marshal arrested him assuming he had stolen the merchandise. However, he had purchased it with a prescription and had left by way of the alley to keep from having to divide it with others. As the editor of the *Democrat* noted that was a "liberal prescription," while the prospect of others waiting to share his largesse pointed to other problems. Even more to the point, the prescription had been written by an area doctor and pretty much authorized the individual, a noted problem drinker, regular access to whiskey, though for no more than a gallon at a time. Another means of avoiding enforcement developed with the formation of a "funnel club" at the location previously occupied by the Club Bar. Under this arrangement, a group would buy a keg of beer and settle in the club room with beer and other provisions. This was legal as one of the members had a wholesale license which permitted him to buy beer by the keg and the case.[41]

Such practices together with actual violations of the dry laws prompted a concerted response by the law enforcement league. These included strengthening the organization throughout the town and county, adding to at least seventy-six members it had reported at the end of January 1908. By this time, L. W. had begun reporting saloon closings and other gains. Beyond general publicity, the committee became increasingly involved in political efforts and efforts to augment enforcement. Their political efforts helped produce a Republican slate as "dry as snuff" in the city election. The Democrats ran three wet candidates along with one dry. In the April city elections, the drys gained, but Marks shortly thereafter reported a "blind tiger bar" at the Eagles lodge and continuing reports of bootlegging and joint openings.

In June, the law enforcement council met with prosecuting attorney J. B. McGilvray urging improved enforcement. McGilvray responded with a public statement later that month. He noted general dissatisfaction with the performance of his office but argued that he was more than willing to prosecute liquor cases if he had evidence. He then issued a challenge to an unidentified group, probably the law enforcement league, who had claimed their attorney advised them they had enough evidence for prosecution. McGilvray told them if their attorney was so convinced, he would deputize him to give him the power of the state to proceed stipulating only that he would not permit anyone to pile up costs against the county.[42]

Four weeks later, the league had not responded to that challenge but had decided to try and garner the quality of evidence McGilvray required. Accordingly, the league employed a detective from Fort Scott under L. W.'s guidance. Those efforts produced a number of arrests and subsequent prosecutions. A grand jury empaneled in September produced less satisfying results. Marks asserted it was dominated by wets, and the jury was unable to reach a decision, delaying resolution until January. That session then issued only one indictment though it led to a subsequent conviction.[43]

Meanwhile Marks' interest in the issue had seemed to wane. That probably reflected his sense that the league group had accomplished its principal goals and he showed little enthusiasm for other measures. He and the committee had also stirred a campaign to enforce Sunday closing laws, but this proposal never gained the momentum the liquor issue had. Both the *Republican* and *Democrat* printed a three-column editorial by G. R. Walser which labeled that proposal as a challenge to American freedom. The editor of the *Democrat,*,which had been initially supportive of Marks and the league, also noted problems with enforcement. There was even less newspaper support as some voices called for other moral laws. One county resident, for instance, had protested the appearance of a woman in pink tights at the opera house. L.W. made no comment about that matter or other moral concerns of the time from opposing use of tobacco to restrictions on movie going, dancing, dominoes, and other games.[44]

Moralism and resultant political tensions would soon break the Democratic hold on the Missouri governorship and other areas of state politics. Holy Joe Folks was defeated in his bid to move from the governorship to the U. S. Senate, and Missourians elected a Republican to replace him. At least some of that defeat was attributed to his "puritanical" reputation.

Baptists were divided less by Folks' moralism than others in Missouri. Folks was more than welcome at the associational meeting held at Lamar, and Baptists remained strong supporters of many of the ideas he was associated with long after he had passed from the political scene.[45] Correspondingly, there were regular resolutions at the Missouri Baptist Convention calling for implementation and enforcement of varied moral reforms which were then advocated with varying degrees of success in churches across the state then and in later years.

The annual meetings of the General Association regularly heard and frequently endorsed a wide variety of resolutions that critics then and to this day might label as puritanical. The Baptist version of the social gospel meant the use of "any good method" to control vice. They also heard calls for support of children's homes, care for the aged, and promoting social justice. Some issues would trigger debates and even divisions, but for the most part, they did not divert Baptists from their primary focus on individual salvation. Even the most devoted advocate of social gospel ideas among Baptists was likely to believe social change offered only temporary and partial solutions to the fundamental problems of individuals. In contrast, they believed conversion produced changed lives leading to positive social change as well as salvation for eternity. Accordingly, Baptists continued to focus on revivals, establishment of new churches and tract ministries. They were increasingly urban, and the issues they addressed and techniques they employed reflected the new challenges they faced, but they remained primarily committed to the goal of individual conversion.[46]

Newspaper accounts of the era regularly reported on mission emphases of the meetings rather than moral issues. One such report from 1908 could very well have been based on the notes L.W. had taken at the annual meeting the prior year. He listed individual officers, budgetary matters, and provided a schedule of events and speakers. He reported extensively on a report of missions work in Brazil, Africa, China, and home mission fields and patterns of support making up four and one-half of the five pages of hand written notes, concluding that section with the following: "The meeting was harmonious, enthusiastic, purposeful. Oh! I want my people to have part in the work."[47]

L. W. reflected the moral climate of the era and regularly gave "strong sermons" to preaching against varied moral issues. However, none of the hundreds of sermons in his files reveal concentration on any such issue other than prohibition. He had urged one minister he counseled to quit smoking, and similarly, he supported church teachings against dancing but always returned to the "positive truths." His own practices included attendance at the opera house and movies, and he enjoyed dominoes, though he was more cautious about card playing. Even when a furor was raised about a local merchant's give away, seen as gambling by many, Marks noted the furor in his diary but made no comment as he often did with issues he was less concerned with. Interestingly, the winner had been one of the dry leaders and probably a wife of a member of his church.[48]

As a result of his continuing focus on the heart of the gospel message, Marks even felt free enough to mingle with religious and other groups that would have been scrupulously avoided by other Baptists. He had dinner with one family he identified as "rank--holiness come-outers" but seemed content to define his differences. And, in early 1909, he even agreed to preach a message on request from a local socialist group, accepting the challenge to preach on the text they had selected. The text was Isaiah 65:21-25, dealing with prophecies of a utopian future when lion and lamb would like down together while all enjoyed prosperity and peace.

Throughout his ministry, L. W. would maintain the practice of attending worship with different churches, and in all of his notes, there was only one occasion when he rejected the possibility of future participation in a group's worship. That occurred with a group of "Campbellites" he believed were characterized by "a lot of rotten stuff." He then proclaimed, "I go back no more." His focus on positive truths also meant that he never allowed his community or social efforts or even his constant struggles to provide for his family to keep him from responding to the needs of individuals whether from his congregation or otherwise. The family kept a young girl for a time before she could be taken in by the Baptist Orphans' Home, and he could always find some money to assist those with greater need, black or white.[49]

In June 1908, Marks was honored by his alma mater, William Jewell College, with a request to dedicate a unique collection the school had obtained. Three years earlier, William Jewell trustees and the college president had arranged for the purchase of the private library of Charles Haddon Spurgeon, the English Baptist and one of the most highly regarded preacher-orators of the era. His library consisted of thousands of books from the 15th century onward as well as contemporary sources. The public ceremony followed years of fund-raising and other arrangements before the books were received at William Jewell.

Marks' notes from his presentation referenced Acts 8:2 for a text and the burial of the martyred Stephen. The lecture provided the major details of Spurgeon's life and some background for the collection. Besides praising the qualities of Spurgeon's preaching, Marks discussed the work he did for orphanages, helpless women, and the establishment of a pastor's college. He also praised him for his role in the downgrade controversy, "one of his greatest works for God, a bold, firm stand against the drift from the Bible and doctrine of the atonement." Marks concluded with an illustration pointing to the potential impact of books and described a process whereby individuals could donate to support of the collection.[50]

The Lamar church continued to grow and prosper during the remainder of his tenure but a few problems began to emerge during his second year there. He reported he was ashamed of the January 1908 missions collection and began noting a number of financial problems that spring and the church began to fall behind on his salary. By October, that deficit had reached $114.50, and the church owed another $35.00 to a custodian and others. In the meantime, L. W. and others attempted to address the growing problem. One deacon's comments about the issue produced a division among the deacons. They divided further over whether or not the church should grant a letter to those who were behind on their pledges. That question troubled Marks and the deacons for two full months before the individual in question paid the amount he had pledged, leaving the other issue moot.[51]

By November, Marks believed that financial matters at the church were "looking up." The deacons had developed a new budget, and there was optimism about the church's commitment to it. By that time, the deficit in collections for the pastor's salary and other bills had been reduced. As the year ended, however, something seemed to destroy that hope. Marks described a "long, complicated discussion" of church finances with three individuals determined to cut the budget by reducing the pastor's salary.[52]

The church caught up on all money due him by the middle of January, but then began falling behind again. In the absence of evidence of major financial problems in the community and continuing growth, four explanations are offered for the growing problems. First, the pattern of financial shortfalls had developed during the height of Marks' reform efforts and probably reflected some members' dissatisfaction with his role in the campaign. If so, those opponents were not likely to support him even after he adopted a lower political profile.

Second, developments in 1909 seemed to support Marks' earlier evaluation that a "hard shell" element was emerging within the deacons and the congregation.[53] In this instance, he used that phrase to define those who tended to drag against church spending. Most of this element did not believe in tithing and were also resistant to changes in programs even when there were not major costs. Development of a cradle roll, the support of a town mission, and calls for other missionary contributions or support of revivals were guaranteed to alienate most if not all of these people. In turn, there were often the core elements in a third group, the traditional group of deacons and other church leaders who were prone to resist any leadership rather than their own. Still others may have been learned of his visits to other congregations in view of a call.

Marks resigned his pastorate in April 1909 partly in response to these pressures, but his decision had already been shaped by an old dream and a new call to return to Oklahoma and lead a new campaign for the *Word & Way*. In May 1908, he agreed to travel to Sapulpa, Oklahoma in view of a call. He enthused about prospects in that booming community of 8,000 people and a church with 200 members and a strong Sunday school despite some organizational problems. He then traveled to Oklahoma City for a three-day associational meeting where he

encountered S. M. Brown of the *Word & Way*. Brown and
Oklahoma Baptist leaders urged him to take up the
campaign anew. The enthusiastic responses he received
convinced him the time was riper than ever before for the
paper in Oklahoma, but he delayed a decision.[53]

He then journeyed to Edmond where he still owned
two lots and then returned to Lamar. The next week, a
visitor from the Sapulpa church attended services at
Lamar, reporting a probable call from Sapulpa. That never
came, and Marks decided against *Word & Way's* proposal.
In October 1908, he completed sale of his lots in Edmond
and reported a good deal on a house in Lamar. That
Edmond deal foundered because of a title problem, but he
still closed on the Lamar property at the end of the month
despite renewed pleas from S. M. Brown.[55]

Brown was not to be denied, however, and came to
visit L. W. at his Lamar home. They talked about
Oklahoma, and L. W. then agreed to consider a return to
Oklahoma to open a branch office for *Word & Way*. The
contractual details were not reported immediately, and
there may have been some disagreement. For the next two
months, he continued his now reduced political efforts and
conducted a revival and other church business. He was
growing increasingly irritable about finances, reporting a
meeting where the church leaders "chewed the rag" as
usual before deciding to try and raise $50.00. A campaign
in early April produced slightly more than one-half that
goal. The same week, L. W.'s favored slate elected the
mayor and town marshal but lost the races for collector
and three alderman positions.[56]

On April 9, Marks reported he felt so bad he could not
work on his sermon so spent the day cutting rags to make
into a rug. Besides his discouragement about church
finances and possibly the election, Marks had fought

recurring battles with his eyes through the preceding year. So, it is possible that a combination of those factors accounted for his ailing. He was slightly encouraged after hearing some good preaching at the Presbyterian Church but responded quickly with the next contact from Brown. On Thursday, April 15, Brown requested that he go to Oklahoma as soon as possible. Marks recorded, "I go Monday."

---

1. Marks' diaries, January – July 1905, passim.

2. Marks' diaries, August 8, 1905.

3. Marks' diaries, June 6 and 8, August 8 and 9, and October 2, 1905.

4. Marks' diaries, June 6 and October 26, 1905.

5. Untitled notes for speech to Edmond GAR post, May 28, 1905, Sermon files, Marks Collection.

6. Undated outline for speech on "A Day of Memories," Sermon files, Marks Collection.

7. Marks' diaries, October 14, 17, 19, and 28, and November 2, 1905.

8. Danney Gobel, *Progressive Oklahoma* (Norman, OK: OU Press, 1980) 212; Dora Ann Stewart, *Government and Development of Oklahoma Territory* (Harlow Publishing Co., 1933) 316.

9. *Progressive Oklahoma* 212; Jimmie Franklin, *Born Sober: Prohibition in Oklahoma, 1907-1959* (Norman, OK: OU Press, 1971) 10; Marks' diaries, June 22, 1905 and May 20, June 12 and 14 and July 1, 1906.

10. "The Land of Beautiful Homes," Marks' miscellaneous writings, Marks Collection.

11. Marks' diaries, June 22, 1905; May 20, June 12 and 14, and July 1, 1906.

12. *Progressive Oklahoma* 212-213.

13. Reports, BGCO, November 1906; Marks' diaries, November 7-10, 1906.

14. Reports, BGCO, November 7-10, 1906; Marks' diaries, November 7-10, 1906; Gaskin. *Baptist Milestones in Oklahoma* 39-150.

15. Marks' diaries, July 17-19 and November 7-10, 1906.

16. *Baptist Milestones in Oklahoma* 49-51.

17. Marks' diaries, March 20-21, April 13-15 and 25-27, 1905.

18 Marks' diaries, July 7 and 12, 1905 and January 22 24, 1906.

19. Marks' diaries, April 9, 10, 25, and 30, May 1, 15 and 16, June 16, 19, 20, 22, and July 2 and 3, 1906.

20. Marks' diaries, July 2, 3 and 25-26 and September 17-18, 1906.

21. Marks' diaries, March 27, May 24-25, and April 17, 1906.

22. Marks' diaries, January 11, February 24, March 3, and May 10-11, 1906.

23. FBC Edmond minutes, June 4, January 31, March 15, May 2, 1906, FBC Edmond.

24. Marks' diaries, April 5, June 10, July 5, 24, 25, 29 and 31, 1906.

25. Marks' diaries, August 24, 1906 and 1-30, passim.

26. Marks' diaries, August 24, 1906 and 1-30, passim.

27. Marks' diaries, September 19 and December 14 and 15, 1906.

28. Marks' diaries, October–November, passim, and December 22-31, 1906.

29. Lamar Leader, January 3, 1907; Marvin Van Gilder, The Story of Barton County (Van Gilder, 1972) 30.

30. Marks' diaries, May 11 and September 26, 1907; March 3, 30, June 16, July 18 and 27, September 7 and November 9, 1908.

31. Marks' diaries, December 15, March 19, and December 29, 1907.

32. *Lamar Democrat*, February 27, 1908; Marks' diaries, February 25-26 and March 10, 1908; Paulette Orahood, Barton Co. Historical Society to Alvin Turner, July 25, 2008.

33. Marks' diaries, January – March 1907, passim, and April 4, 1907.

34. Marks' diaries, March 3, April 23, May 11 and 15, July 7, August 7, December 31, 1907 and April 12 and May 3, 1908.

35. Marks' diaries, March 1 and 5 and April, passim and September 13, 1907 and June 24, 1908.

36. James J. Connolly, review of Steven L. Piott, *Holy Joe: Joseph W. Folks and the Missouri Idea* (U. of Missouri Press, 1998) as published on H-Net Review:, h-net.org/reviews, March 1999.

37. Ibid; *Frontiers* 107.

38. *Lamar Leader,* February 7, April 18, 1907; Marks' diaries, October 5, 8, 9, and 10-14, 1907.

39. Marks' diaries, November 1907, passim, and December 13, 1907.

40. Marks' diaries, January 9, 11, 16, 18, 24, February 10, March 16 and 30, 1908; *Lamar Democrat*, January 2, 16, 23, 30 and February 6 and 13, 1908.

41. *Lamar Democrat*, June 25, 1908, Marks' diaries, April 24, May 13, 22, 23 and 28, June 8 and 9 and July 1-14, 1908.

42. *Lamar Democrat*, June 25,26 and July 16,1908; Marks' diaries, March 20, April 24 and May 23, 1908.

43. *Lamar Democrat*, June 25, 1908; Marks' diaries, June 9, July 1-14, August 21 and September 14-19, 1908 and January 12 and 16, 1909.

44. *Lamar Republican*, May 9 and 14, 1908; *Lamar Democrat*, April 20 and May 7, 1908.

45. Marks' diaries, October 15, 1908.

46. *Frontiers* 99-105.

47. Moberly, *Missouri Weekly,* October 18, 1907 and October 23, 1908; the Ada, *Oklahoma Evening News*, October 22, 1909; Marks' notes from unidentified 1907 association meeting, October 22, 1907, Marks miscellaneous writings, Marks Collection.

48. Marks' diaries, March 7, 1908.

49. Marks' diaries, March 15, 1909.

50. Undated notes for Spurgeon dedication; Sermon files, Marks' Collection: Marks' diaries, June 27-28, 1908.

51. Marks' diaries, January 2, April 2, June 18 and 21, July 26 and 30, August 1, October 29, November 5 and 17 and December 31, 1908.

52. Marks' diaries, November 17 and December 31, 1908.

53. Marks' diaries, June 18, 1908.

54. Marks' diaries, May 14-22 and 31, 1908.

55. Ibid.

56. Marks' diaries, March 31, April 1, 4, and 6, 1909.

Chapter 5

Home Again—The Return To Oklahoma

Marks' return to Oklahoma can only be understood with reference to his progressive goals for Baptist work in the new state. The church at Lamar offered security and relative prosperity as well as the potential to continue influencing the life of that community. In contrast, however, Oklahoma offered a larger venue with much Baptist work still in formative stages. This was particularly evident in the case of the two primary items on Marks' progressive agenda. Oklahoma Baptist College still struggled with debt and erratic support compounded by new competitors for limited Baptist funds. Moreover, there was still no newspaper serving Baptists statewide. For Marks this meant denominational work, and church members in Oklahoma remained in imminent danger of becoming lopsided.

At the same time, he had come to love Oklahoma in other respects. He had grown to love the state and hoped to nurture the seeds of the gospel and progressive values there. He would face numerous disappointments in the next few years but never seemed to regret his decision to return. Similarly, as many of his dreams died, he retained his commitment to the values that motivated his work. He spent a week in Oklahoma in mid April visiting Baptist leaders, writing letters to ministers across the state, and making arrangements for an Oklahoma City office. The

latter plans were delayed by some confusion at the *Word &
Way* home office, so he did not establish an office or a
concentrated sales effort until July. His resumed his Marks
Remarks columns in the paper shortly following much the
same format for other Oklahoma material as they had
previously. This changed the following June when the
paper eliminated a separate column for Oklahoma. The
new format focused on "denominational life and work,"
though Marks continued his regular columns focusing on
aspects of work in Oklahoma, and actual content changed
little. There were promotions for the children's home,
Oklahoma Baptist College, and other Baptist work. The
paper also offered frequent encouragement to BGCO's
promotion of missions and to continuing prohibition
battles, with the state facing the first of many subsequent
challenges to its constitutional restrictions on the sale of
alcoholic beverages. By this time also, the national debate
on prohibition was increasing soon to result in the passage
of the 18*th* Amendment to the U. S. Constitution providing
for national prohibition in 1919.[1]

As before, Marks preached and taught in workshops,
attended association meetings, promoted the OBC, and
raised funds for the orphanage. His continuing advocacy
of varied progressive ideas also led him to near comic
efforts to use a motorcycle to travel the state. In the July 7,
1910 issue of *Word & Way*, Marks proclaimed the
"Evolution of Locomotion" announcing his acquisition of
a motorcycle and related plans.

The Evolution of Locomotion

Nearly half a century this scribe has been using various
contrivances for getting from place to place. From the
stick horse to a bareback ride on the family mare was a
long jump successfully made at about 3 years of age.
Later on came the gunny sack saddle and the leather
saddle. The two horse team or the four horse team to

the big wagon, sleighs in winter and buggies in summer have come and gone.

In the twenty years since the little country church said go preach the gospel we have, in the interest of that gospel, used about all of the contrivances of locomotion known to this latitude from the primitive shanks' ponies, which the Irishman pronounced the cheapest and safest," on up, or down, as the case may be.

We have gone horseback, in buggy and trains and steamboats, but now in the state that must have the best, with the paper that trails after nothing in its line, in the service of the Baptist people who deserve the best service, we are riding the fastest thing out.

A new four-horse power Harley-Davidson motor cycle is the latest acquisition to the Word and Way's equipment for prompt and good service. We are riding it over these fine prairie roads in Oklahoma.

The Motor Cycle is about the present limit for speed. "How fast can it go?" is the standard question. Well, I don't know, a mile a minute, perhaps. But I don't ride that fast, thank you. Twenty or twenty-five miles an hour will do for me. It can outrun a street car or railroad train. It can run around an automobile and make it interesting for a jack rabbit.

In our independent move from house to house and from town to town, we are developing a supreme indifference to three cent railroad fare and a growing contempt for inconvenient schedules of railroads. The fact is we have quit ridin' on the kars.

With our eye upon the road our best hand on the throttle and a grip upon nerve we are gone. Lookout for us we are liable to come puffing up to your door at any time. Have your dollar ready, for the Word and Way, the paper of enterprise and prompt service.[2]

He had never acquired a horse and buggy in Oklahoma, walking, riding trolleys or trains as needed and he often reported walking as much as five miles when connections were missed or not available, so his purchase seemed practical. He spent a week learning to ride it and then took a round trip from his home in northwestern Oklahoma City to Britton, making the trip in thirty-seven minutes from his office in the Indian Building at the corner of First and Robinson with no trouble. The next few days, however, presented unanticipated difficulties as he ventured on to rural roads. Besides problems with the unpaved and even ungraded roads, his bike proved unable to climb some hills, and he once had to have it hauled two miles to get through some sand and at another time to cross a river. He also faced continuing difficulties finding gasoline. By August, a series of such incidents along with a number of flats and a blow out made him decide to leave his "wheel" in Kingfisher and take a train to Hennessey. A similar series of problems later in the month, plus continuing problems of rain and wind as the next few finally forced him to put it aside in October. He tried to ride it at least one time during November but made no subsequent references to the motorcycle.[3]

Despite that disappointing experience, Marks retained his fascination with modernization. For instance, he would commend Pastor George Sherman of Chickasha for buying an auto in 1911. Marks wrote: "We applaud when Baptist pastors can have modern conveniences," asserting that they were necessities, not luxuries and would prove cheaper than a horse and buggy. Marks would not be able to purchase his own car until 1916.

Marks dedicated the better part of the next three years of his life to establishing the *Word & Way* as one means to promote the goals he had identified in his song. It would prove to be an unprofitable venture for both the newspaper and Marks personally. While his work for the paper provided the foundation for significant contributions in other areas of Oklahoma Baptist life, it never met either his financial needs or professional goals.

The financial problems stemmed from a set of interconnected problems. At best, Oklahoma Baptists were not likely to fund the costs of a newspaper. As Marks wrote in another context, Oklahomans remained "hard run" as they had been during his previous sojourn. In 1909, Oklahoma's economy remained significantly behind national trends with per capita income below 60% of the national norm despite phenomenal annual growth in Oklahoma City and Tulsa, with the latter just then beginning to burgeon from impact of the oil discoveries at nearby Glenn Pool. Those urban areas and even Edmond stood in sharp contrast to the grinding poverty characteristic of much of the state's farmers and even the small towns that served them. For those people, $1.00 per year for a subscription to the *Word & Way* represented enough of a cost to be seen as a luxury. These inherent problems were compounded by a regional drought which would disrupt the state's economy until 1913.

Most Oklahomans also tended to be suspicious of the literary qualities and progressive qualities of the *Word & Way*. For instance, Marks describes one association as a pocket of poverty. The same association continued to endorse D. B. Ray's *Baptist Flag* even though it had virtually ceased publication by this time. Even facing these disadvantages, Marks reported sending in more than 1,000 new subscriptions by the end of 1909, and the following June, he reported 752 new subscriptions in eleven months. These gains were not adequate to sustain his paper for long in Oklahoma, and the environment grew worse the next year.[4]

The *Word & Way's* inherent disadvantages were increased by ambiguous actions and periods of passivity at the Kansas City office. Management was determined not to push the paper "without regard to the wishes of the brethren." They would emphasize their tranquility, making "no trouble for the brethren of Oklahoma . . ."[5] This left the vast majority of the work undertaken in Oklahoma on the shoulders of L. W. Marks. It also meant that he operated with no budget for advertising and was expected to generate enough income to offset most of those costs. Specifically, that meant raising salaries and expenses of $1,500 annually to be met by the revenue from new subscription sales and twenty five percent of the stock he might sell.[6]   The expense allowance soon proved inadequate, although Marks continued to offset some costs boarding with pastors or families among the congregations he contacted. A contract adjustment addressed this problem while his work ethic and other assets made up for other deficiencies in 1909. However, as before, the home office never seemed particularly concerned about Marks' need for regular income. It is also apparent that *Word & Way* management regularly failed to honor a contract provision calling for some subsidy of Marks' efforts, instead compensating him almost exclusively on the basis of the income he generated.

In reality, these experiences were virtually interchangeable with Marks' and the *Word & Way's* previous venture into Oklahoma. That observation leads inevitably to the question: why did either expect things to be different in 1909? The answer is relatively simple. Both had received encouragement and assurance from Baptist leaders throughout the state that this time, the time was ripe, and they wanted to believe that it was. S. M. Brown and others at *Word & Way* believed in their paper and shared Marks' hope of sustaining a progressive voice in the new state. And, the initial responses to the new venture seemed to justify their hopes.   Even with the confused beginning in April 1909, Marks' early efforts for the paper were most successful. After writing letters to twenty-two Oklahoma and Missouri Baptist leaders as the first step toward increasing the stockholder base, he first traveled to Bartlesville where he sold $500 in stock and then to Oklahoma City.[7]

During the following week in the City, he visited with Joseph (J. C.) Stalcup on two different occasions. Stalcup had served as corresponding secretary of the Baptist General Convention of Indian Territory from 1903-1906. He had supported the merger with the Oklahoma Baptist State Convention enthusiastically and became the first corresponding secretary of the BGCO, the body formed from that unification. Stalcup was later recognized as the "great unifier" for Oklahoma Baptists and actively promoted education and a Baptist newspaper for the state.[8]

Marks personally admired Stalcup and regarded his tenure as a "credit to himself and . . . the convention." He went on to assert that "The unparalleled growth of Baptists in the state is due in large measure to the generalship of this consecrated layman and uncompromising Baptist." L.W. was especially pleased by his second meeting with Stalcup, but the corresponding secretary was also an advocate for a "good, religious, up-to-date Baptist newspaper printed and published in the state . . ." The key words in that phrase as they affected *Word & Way* interests were the last four.[9]

Moreover, Stalcup's call for a Baptist paper had led to another distressing result. This came with the establishment of the *Baptist Worker* by Alonzo Nunnery who was then pastor of the First Baptist Church at Granite. He later moved his paper to Chickasha where he also ministered as a bi-vocational pastor. Nunnery was an advocate of Landmark ideas and in many other respects carried on the divisive and confrontational policies of D. B. Ray, though he would steer clear of conflict for the next few years.

Other publishing efforts arose even as the *Word & Way* reentered the Oklahoma market. Marks mentioned the first of these in September 1909. He never noted the name of this paper but described the promoter as a "blow hard —who made great promises with little prospect of keeping them." Nevertheless, the new paper managed to sell some subscriptions and stock as well during the next few months before abandoning the effort. Its success, however, pointed to the continuing goal of many Oklahomans for a Baptist paper printed within the state. While this one effort had little direct impact on the *Word & Way's* successes and it probably added increasing suspicion of all newspaper ventures, the real problem remained the issue of state identify.[10]

The *Baptist Worker* benefitted from that interest as did one other paper Marks referred to during 1909, though again without mentioning its name. Marks also mentioned a Baptist Journal and another unidentified Baptist paper trying to gain an audience located at Enid.   By this time, the *Baptist Flag* had almost ceased publication. Dr. Ray had alienated many of his prior supporters and had to be called down for ranting at the 1910 BGCO annual meeting despite the fact he was speaking for temperance, an issue supported by one and all.

The *Word & Way's* status changed noticeably during the next year with Marks' diaries reflecting growing concern about the entry of Dr. A. J. Holt and the *Baptist Oklahoman* after the summer of 1910. While "feeling bad" about the competition, L.W. seemed just as worried about the venture's potential to harm Dr. Holt. Marks knew Holt, who had been a missionary to the Seminoles, and had worked with him in a number of capacities. He admired Holt and supported him for election as presiding officer at the annual meetings of the convention from 1910 to 1912. By September 1910, L. W. would report that Stalcup and other leaders were promoting the *Oklahoman*, effectively eliminating Marks' ability to sell subscriptions or stock. Stalcup's promotion of the *Baptist Oklahoman* seems to contradict his earlier encouragement to S. M. Brown and Marks. However, he had always advocated a state paper and had followed through on his promises to *Word & Way* before the *Baptist Oklahoman* entered the field.[11]

By that time, Stalcup may have decided that the *Word & Way* would not meet the state's needs. Even more important, under Baptist polity, the ultimate decisions in such matters were rooted in the local congregations, not executive offices. Stalcup could recommend and encourage, but he could not establish policy. This may explain why neither Marks nor Brown seemed to feel any sense of betrayal from Stalcup's actions. Neither did either indicate they received any apologies or explanation from Stalcup. Marks' woes were compounded in the next two months. In October, he reported that President Moore of Oklahoma Baptist College was promoting the *Oklahoman*. The situation worsened the next month in conjunction with the 1910 annual meeting of the BGCO which reflected a strong sentiment for a state paper, ultimately endorsing the *Oklahoman*.[12]

Marks continued to refrain from any adverse comments about Holt but responded sharply in his diary about an offer to join the *Oklahoman*. Later that month, he labeled the paper "a wildcat scheme; still later he rejected another offer to sell subscriptions, writing that "I feel indignant." Marks' assessment of the *Baptist Oklahoman*, and the potential impact on Dr. Holt would prove prescient the next year.[13]

The action of the 1911 state convention, however, seemed to point to a different fate for Holt's paper. A committee of that convention proclaimed their belief in a "Baptist age." That only required "wholesome, vigorous, high-toned progressive literature." They specifically linked that spirit to a new Baptist apologetic that was emerging in the writing of progressive Baptists such as E. Y. Mullins, the president of Southern Seminary. Marks almost certainly would have applauded those statements and subsequent language pertaining to the value of Baptist newspapers which were needed to foster the growth of that spirit, to make "whole Baptists out of half Baptists, strong Baptists out of weak Baptists, working Baptists out of idle Baptists." He was not as happy about the rest of the committee's action.[14]

The committee then went on to give the strongest possible endorsement to the *Baptist Oklahoman*. Their report recognized the valuable services rendered by "good Baptist papers of other states circulated within our borders" but asserted, "These can never take the place of a good state paper." The *Baptist Oklahoman* had "signally served us, . . . hastening every step of our denominational progress. It has powerfully seconded every appeal that our leaders have made." The committee then went on to call for financial and moral support of a denominational paper. The committee referenced considerable study of the issues but had somehow missed the most glaring problem. Even as the convention was meeting, Marks was reporting the demise of the *Baptist Oklahoman*. Marks would report the paper's bankruptcy at the end of November. At the same time, he mourned that Dr. Holt had been ruined financially by the failure of the paper, "a sad thing."[15]

Marks' sadness reflected both his concern for Dr. Holt and for the status of Oklahoma Baptist newspapers. Following the 1910 convention, *Word & Way* had begun to reduce its sales efforts in Oklahoma. S. M. Brown had been present at the 1910 convention but chose not to challenge the endorsement of the *Baptist Oklahoman* at that time. The following February, the home office asked Marks to accept a reduction in pay, in effect placing him solely on commission for sales and some compensation for his submissions.

Brown remained serene about the Oklahoma venture following the 1910 convention with the declaration "The *Word & Way* is tranquil," celebrating the fact they had served faithfully and made no trouble for Oklahoma. A front page editorial in 1912, probably by Brown, reflected the same sentiment, extended sympathy for Dr. Holt and averred that the author would have rejoiced if Holt had been able to succeed. He then went on to discuss the history of *Word & Way*'s involvement in Oklahoma. He defended *Word & Way's* Oklahoma coverage, highlighting attention given women's work, the orphanage, educational and mission interests. He concluded with a comment defending the value of newspapers to Baptist work. However, he also argued that any future paper had to consider financial realities and failure of all prior efforts in Oklahoma including to some extent that of the *Word & Way*.[16]

Marks echoed many of the same sentiments in his remarks in the same issue. On the economic side, he asserted that a dedicated Oklahoma paper would need to charge at least $2.00 per subscription to fund its costs. Otherwise, it would require convention financial support which Marks opposed. He also cautioned against convention support of publishing attempts by those without newspaper experience noting, "We have spoiled many a good pastor trying to make an editor or denominational man out of him."

The remainder of his arguments reveal his own state of mind as well as his analysis of Oklahoma's newspaper problems:

> The most perplexing of all the perplexing problems that constantly confront Baptist people is the weekly Baptist paper. In this matter we in Oklahoma have suffered many things from many physicians. It is perfectly plain to every one that we are no better, but rather worse, off than before. It is also plain that the physicians and nostrums increase the gravity of the disease.
>
> The dogmatism with which we have been assured that we absolutely must have a state paper, has been equaled only by the positive assurance that the last one to secure the floor knew exactly how to meet the necessity.
>
> The absolute necessity of a state paper has been asserted so often and so emphatically that a good many folks who ought to know better have almost believed it. But there remains a considerable number of right respectable folks who have all along doubted the premise. Why is it necessary for Oklahoma to have a state paper? The answer is at hand, worn so slick by use that few think to question: "It is necessary to unify our people." Any one familiar with Baptist work in Oklahoma can see with their eyes shut that the papers that we have had have produced rather the opposite effect. In the days of Oklahoma Territory, when we recognized no official organ except our secretary's Bulletin, there was more unity of purpose and harmony of action than has been during any of the days when we were attempting to found a state paper.
>
> That the Baptists of a state can do quite respectable work without an official state paper is plainly set forth by our neighbors on the north. Their course in regard to the Baptists paper problem is in striking contrast with our frantic and disastrous plunging at the problem. We have financially ruined a lot of good brothers and advertised our shortage on good business judgment until we must look ridiculous to our neighbors.

> While good men have done their best, even remarkably well under the circumstances, . . . We have put forth such extravagant advertisements of greatness, and unmatched achievements, and then sent forth an official organ . . . that looked like a burlesque on the cause we seek to promote.
>
> We believe in Baptist papers with all our heart, and demonstrate our faith by our works. We believe in good papers, just as good as we can make them. Papers that educate, indoctrinate, and lift up our people and give them a genuine respect for themselves. . . . A paper that stands for all of our Baptist people, and all of our Baptist enterprises.
>
> The seat of orthodoxy and center of soundness, among Baptists, is the people. If the people are given a fair chance they will support that which is good and reject the bad. . . .
>
> That the imaginary lines that bound a state should bound the circulation of a paper looks to this writer like it is not according to good business sense nor Baptist principles.[17]

Marks continued occasional columns for *Word & Way* for the remainder of the year, and the paper sent a representative to the 1912 convention but ended most Oklahoma reporting in the spring of 1913. In the meantime, state Baptists awaited a man with "a bushel of brains and barrel of money" to give them another paper. They got half of that when C. P. Stealey began the *Baptist Messenger* in the spring of 1912. Stealey did not have the capital Marks believed was necessary but soon built a substantial subscription base, partly due to Marks' efforts.

Stealey defined his goals as creating a "newsy, spiritual and constructive" paper that would stand squarely on verbal inspiration of the Bible . . . "gathering the saved into spiritual churches where they may be trained and developed in the work of making more believers and more churches." He had no sympathy for "the modern cry for union, federation, and cooperation" but recognized that "there are good Christian people in most denominations with whom personally our people can cooperate so many ways."[18]

The latter note helps to explain Marks' ready support of the *Messenger* despite differences on Stealey's premillennial stance and fundamentalist tendencies. L. W. was one of the two speakers who gave a "splendid" speech on behalf of the new newspaper at the Central Association meeting in September 1912. The next year, he promoted a convention-wide effort to boost Stealey's paper calling for pastors to help enroll subscribers with the goal of reaching one-hundred new subscribers the first year. He then headed that effort, launching the campaign with a full page editorial in the *Messenger*.[19] Later, the convention approved sale of Marks' L. L. Smith biography at a reduced rate to new subscribers.

Ultimately, such efforts gained 5,000 subscribers to the *Messenger* and it was recognized as the state's unofficial Baptist organ within a few years. In 1919, its status became official when the convention purchased the paper from Stealey for $5,000, retaining him as editor in part to offset increasing attacks from Nunnery's *Baptist Worker*. Ironically, Stealey would be dismissed from his position in 1928 for "his trouble-making spirit of contention and disharmony among the brethren" of state Baptist leadership at that time.[20]

The financial history of the *Baptist Messenger* and Stealey's eagerness to sell it in 1919 support much of Marks' arguments about the economic realities facing the promoters of an Oklahoma-based paper. The *Messenger's* financial struggles between 1913 and 1919 confirmed his fear that economic realities would necessitate convention support. What he did not anticipate, however, was that the state paper might become a source of contention and disharmony. Despite his long-term experience with D. B. Ray and his knowledge of Nunnery's *Baptist Worker*, Marks and his fellow progressives rarely recognized the fact that new technologies and even education could be used against the values they stood for.

In contrast, Marks' relative equanimity regarding the failure of *Word & Way* is easily explained. His own continuing frustrations with payments from the organization and the ongoing phase out of its Oklahoma operations had given him time to adjust to that reality and to seek alternatives. That meant a pastorate as he had also come to recognize a hard reality; he no longer had either the physical energy to continue working as he had before or the capacity to withstand time away from his family. His letters from 1909 reveal a man in agony. He wrote that he was so lonesome and homesick, "I could cry." He wondered if they could ever be settled again and commented that if he wasn't so busy, "I couldn't stand it." As 1909 drew to a close, he wrote that he closed the year with a thankful heart, affirming that God had sustained him. At the same time, he was homesick for family and ". . . This work is too much for me. I must do something else. Goodbye to 1909. Amen."[21]

He had brought his family to Oklahoma City three months earlier, but days apart from them on the road were more than he could sustain for long. He began to pursue a pastorate in earnest, but as had occurred on other such occasions, he had a number of encouraging responses, but none led to a full-time call. He began preaching quarter-time at Fletcher in November, continuing there at least until March 1910. In July, he finally accepted a half-time call from the Banner Church, west of Oklahoma City, after regular supply work there the preceding three months. The next month, he began writing casualty insurance with the first of a series of companies he would work for during the next few years. These income sources plus some continuing pay from *Word & Way* gave him a steady, though minimal, income. He was still hoping for a full-time call at the end of the year, but that prayer would not be answered in the affirmative until the end of 1912.[21]

Diminishing income from *Word & Way* and irregular payments from the Banner Church frequently left him with the cash flow problems which by this time had become a constant in his life. In January 1911, he received only fifty cents from the church which he characterized as "pretty tough when a fellow is so hard run and winter time too." To compensate, he began selling property insurance which led to limited financial gains and opened new prospects for this future. Even as his insurance business grew, L. W. Marks continued his work for the paper and on behalf of the children's home, association programs and OBC.

As before, he consulted with the children's home's leadership on a regular basis, meeting with J. A. Scott, the first superintendent and his successor W. A. McKinney to encourage them and promoting attention to its needs through the *Word & Way*. For instance, in May 1911, he reported on a decision of the Sunday school at Carmen to donate one offering monthly to the home while the Salt Fork Association had passed a resolution urging church-wide offerings to benefit the home on every month with a fifth Sunday. In all likelihood, these activities reflected L. W.'s inspiration and encouragement. He went on to propose that one-hundred Oklahoma churches accept the challenge of the Salt Creek and Carmen actions.[23]

He raised funds regularly for the home along with OBC as he attended associational meetings and promoted

Word & Way. In most instances, he received no payment for the collections except for a brief period during 1911 when he launched a sustained effort for the orphanage to avert a crisis caused by economic woes in the state. During the same period, McKinney traveled the state, raising an average of $50 monthly to support the orphanage but still fell short of its needs. In January 1911, Marks reported he was on the road for the home and his financial calculations for the year show a small amount received for the home. Later that year, he took a two-week trip to the panhandle to raise money for the orphanage. He had only eleven cents when he arrived but collected $5.00 on *Word & Way* subscriptions to meet the needs that were not provided by area church members or other supporters. He then raised as much as $157.00 in cash plus notes during August and another $388.00 in September 1911, a significant portion of the home's immediate needs.[24]

Marks' help during this crucial period undoubtedly helped insure the home's survival and. It remained close to his heart for the remainder of his ministry. He was always ready to give, encourage others to do so, and he and Mrs. Marks regularly hosted children from the home at church and in their own home. The home's long struggle for survival finally ended in 1915, when the BGCO began to assume full responsibilities for its expenses.

Associational work represented much more than occasions for marketing or fund-raising to Marks. He believed in their work and delighted in interaction with his fellow Baptists. He continued to enjoy hearing preaching and accepted every possible invitation to teach or preach. Other entertainment, from music to debate, added to his enjoyment. He had even retained his zest for the rigors that were frequently required by such gatherings. Such meetings were often held at rural locations, leaving all except a few church members who might live in the immediate area dependent on neighbors or camping arrangements. These arrangements had one clear advantage for travelers such as Marks who was nearly always short of cash.[25]

On the other hand, local hospitality often presented visitors with other challenges. For instance, on one occasion, he stayed at a nearby Texas ranch when attending a Beaver associational meeting and spent the night warring with bed bugs. L. W. took such problems as a matter of course and could still proclaim camping out in tents or under the stars as a good time. The meetings of the Central Association usually did not offer good times out doors but he continued working tirelessly for the evangelistic programs and other programs it sponsored.[26]

In the meantime, Marks was witnessing the death throes of Oklahoma Baptist College. That result was not expected when Marks returned to Oklahoma in 1909. In fact, the college reported its "best year ever" with 120 students, and completion of some building improvements. The appointment of J. H. Moore as the new president ended four years of flux in that office, with seven different persons holding the title during that time. The next year, the college reported another record enrollment with more than 200 students. In reality, however, serious problems remained, and new ones were developing. Most important, the college had never managed to reduce its debt significantly. A second problem compounded the financial difficulties faced by the administration and trustees. In its simplest form, this was the fact that the college's location meant it could not expect to gain either widespread attendance from potential Baptist students

across Oklahoma or unified support from the convention.
[27]

Even if that goal had been attained, Oklahoma Baptists were stretched by demands from varied other institutions and projects they supported, and that difficulty was worsened by statewide economic problems. Nevertheless, the convention added to their difficulties by actions taken from 1910-1912. In 1910, they agreed to begin helping support the Southwest Baptist Academy. Even with that support, the school's financial problems forced its removal from Hastings to Mangum in 1912. It would function at that location for the next three years as Western Baptist College before it ceased operation in 1915.[28]

That school was actually more of a prep-school than a college, but it added to the convention's financial obligations while further fragmenting its support of education. In the meantime, the convention started yet another college. In 1907, the Education Commission of the BGCO reported on Baptist educational efforts in Oklahoma and declared it "insufficient." This was based on a study that indicated there were at least 700 Baptist young men and women enrolled in the state's secular schools. That led to a recommendation calling for establishment of a new Baptist university. The secretary of the commission then began notifying several cities of the state to submit proposals for location of the college. Nine cities eventually submitted proposals: Lawton, Chickasha, Hobart, Guthrie, El Reno, Blackwell, Oklahoma City, and Shawnee.

The Blackwell proposal, in effect, would have meant locating the new university at the site of Oklahoma Baptist College which would have only replicated the problem the convention had with that site. The Oklahoma

City proposal was another matter but was keyed to support promised by I. N. Putnam, the developer of the area that would become Putnam City. Putnam's presentation, however, had reserved the right to name trustees. The proposals from other towns had other problems and none exceeded the offer from Shawnee. That included an offer of $100,000 plus sixty acres of land for the campus. Accordingly, the commission accepted the Shawnee proposal in 1907 and filed articles of incorporation early the next year.[29]

A building committee for the new university was appointed in June, and a corner stone was laid for the first building in February 1911. Classes had already commenced the preceding September with students meeting at First Baptist Church, Convention Hall, and Shawnee High School. J. M. Carroll was the first president. Marks was among those who met Carroll upon his arrival at Shawnee in April 1910. Carroll died in 1931, at which time a collection of his lectures was published as *The Trail of Blood*, an argument for Baptist secessionism and other Landmark views.[30]

Marks supported the creation of Oklahoma Baptist University (OBU) and attended some of its early organizational meetings as well as cornerstone laying. At the same time, he remained an advocate for OBC in his columns in the *Word & Way* and he had been appointed to the board of that college in 1910. However, his overriding concern was for strengthening Baptist education in the state rather than exclusively at OBC.[31]

An undated sermon from this period summarizes Marks' continuing commitments to higher education. He based the sermon upon II Timothy 2:15, arguing that study was necessary to fulfill Jesus' command to spread the gospel. For Marks, this meant denominational schools to foster training for ministry. In support of that belief, he quoted one source who reported that all but one of the denomination's missionaries to China had been educated in denominational schools. He then went on to argue that "we might do mission work in Oklahoma for a generation and let other folks educate our children, and we would be weaker than we are now. The value of gold is lessened by alloy." He concluded with an argument for supporting current expenses for "our *schools.*"[32]

The creation of another school was consistent with that goal and the convention's proposal had called for continuing support of both OBC and Hastings Baptist College, with OBU having the role as coordinator of Baptist higher education efforts statewide. In truth, both Marks and the educational commission were overly optimistic about state Baptists' capacity to support that scope of work. Before that reality became clear, OBC faced yet more challenges to its existence. In early 1911, Marks reported that both the church and college at Blackwell were in a terrible mess. The pastor had resigned, and the president was at odds with the community.

In February 1911, OBC board members and President Moore met together with the BGCO education commission. Marks then wrote Moore had "betrayed the college," for promoting a new college at "Enid," though later developments would find Moore working on behalf of a proposed college in Oklahoma City. The resultant situation created confusion that compounded continuing funding problems. L. W. and other OBC board members then began developing a number of proposals while meeting with numerous groups in an effort to salvage the college. At first, L. W. was optimistic about a series of meetings at Blackwell with the Commercial Club and others to map out plans for continuing the work there.

They "patched up" one plan to provide for the college's continuance, but it was disrupted by threatened law suits from the company which held some of the mortgages on the college property.[33]

More patching temporarily resolved that immediate problem, but worse lay ahead. At a May 5 board meeting, President Moore announced plans to assume the presidency of Carey Baptist College which was under development in Oklahoma City. The year before, I. N. Putnam had responded to the rejection of his earlier proposal with a plan to create a new college at the site he had originally offered to the convention. Marks reported that the board was indignant about the action.[34]

Marks visited the proposed site of the "extensively advertised" college later in the month and reported there was nothing to be seen other than the land. Nevertheless, others believed it offered a practical solution to the continuing struggles of OBC, if that college could be moved there. At best the Carey college proposal really offered little more than empty promises and gave no attention to either disposition of OBC property at Blackwell or payment of its debt. Still, there were enough backers of President Moore and other Carey College advocates to create a stormy meeting of the OBC board in June. A number of teachers indicated their desire to follow Moore to Oklahoma City at the end of the term. The board agreed to their departure but that left the problem of how to raise funds to support those that remained and identify new teachers and a new president. Eventually, L. W. and W. D. Moorer worked out arrangements leading to organization of a new board and a fund-raising effort in cooperation with the Blackwell Commercial Club.[35]

By July, Marks would indicate that things "looked good" for the college. He spent considerable time in meetings with the new president, Dr. A. E. Bolen, and recruiting for the school. Eventually, 108 students enrolled for the fall, but the college faced enormous challenges. It had closed operations for the prior year with a $3,600 deficit, and the total debt now stood at $35,000. Yet another loan was required to keep the college open in September.

The college's financial needs and varied strategies to resolve them eventually cost L. W. some money and put his reputation at risk. A local insurer agreed to float a loan for the college through his insurance company, but that depended on L. W. and others selling $400,000 worth of life insurance. The insurer then reneged on the deal and also faulted on his payment to *Word & Way* for an ad promoting the venture. L. W. met with the insurance agent in early January after he had written Marks agreeing to pay on the *Word & Way* account. However, he then attacked Marks physically when they met; Marks pushed him off two to three times while shielding his face from the man's blows. A woman screamed and his assailant "came to his senses" and begged forgiveness. They then talked and prayed together. President Bolen then met with the agent and assured Marks the money would be paid, but it never was.[36]

The college managed to stay afloat for the next year, but the end was nearing. Even worse, Baptist work in general and the colleges in particular were facing unprecedented financial pressures. A prolonged meeting in May, probably in the Oklahoma City area, produced a joint operating plan for OBU and OBC. Then at the June 4-5 board meeting and college commencement, the members received the shocking news that classes had been suspended at OBU. President Carroll sold personal possessions to help meet teachers' salaries, but they still received only one-third of the amount they were due while Carroll received only $75.00 toward his contract of $3,000. OBU would eventually rise from the ashes and make Shawnee stand for Oklahoma Baptists "as Jerusalem to the Jews and Athens to the Greeks," but renewal of that institution would wait three more years.[37]

The closing of OBU could have helped OBC except for persistent debt problems and the statewide financial crisis that had forced closing of OBU. The college's doom was sealed when the convention's refused to consider further support of OBC. The college's report to the 1912 convention was headlined: Oklahoma State Baptist in Peril. The author discussed the debt problem and lawsuits that were being "vigorously pushed" to foreclose on $32,000 in debt. There was also another mortgage in the amount of $800 that had property owners threatening to remove all furniture from the building.

The next headline, probably written by Marks or Bolen, summarized the issues: "Baptist Honor Is at Stake." The author called for financial integrity and the fulfillment of promises to donors, students, and other supporters along with the citizens of Blackwell. He argued it was particularly offensive to neglect such commitments even while progress continued toward construction elsewhere. That comment referred to continuing construction of Shawnee Hall on the OBU campus. Finally, he called for Baptists to "wake up, put on their working clothes, and look a great situation squarely in the face. Baptists are not dishonest . . . (and) are not given to the abandonment of a great cause, nor are they in the habit of repudiating honest debts."[38]

The author's pleas did not produce the results hoped for. The Education commission largely ignored the OBC cause, calling for the "establishment of ONE and only one, great, thoroughly equipped coeducational college and that any effort to establish any other be discouraged." The Committee recommended an exception to the policy for Western Baptist College, recommending that it be allowed to continue as a junior college. The action also encouraged the establishment of high grade academies at strategic locations as time and necessity might dictate. OBC was also given a slight endorsement that called for it to become a Baptist college for young women once a university was established.

If that action did not sound the death knell for OBC, the subsequent response to the college's fund-raising effort certainly did. Marks reported only $45.00 raised in a collection to benefit the college at t.he 1912 meeting of the BGCO, President Bolen and the college financial secretary, J. E. Ross, then began another statewide fund-raising campaign. They then hired B. A. Loving to assist with the effort but by June they had to admit failure. They had only raised enough money to meet the current expenses for the year and pay back less than one-half the $3,000 owed faculty from 1911-1912 or a total of about $3,200. The college was then placed in bankruptcy, and the property sold at auction to the Missouri State Life Insurance Co. for $18,000, about $1,500 less than mortgages against the building. Later campaigns raised about one-half of the money owed to faculty and administrators.[39]

Marks had reduced his efforts on behalf of the college significantly during 1912, and he reported no work for it during 1913. This probably reflected a realistic assessment of the college's fate, but it also came in conjunction with his return to the pastorate at the First Baptist Church of Edmond. He would conclude his ministry and spend the rest of his life in that community.

1. Marks' Remarks, April 1909, passim; June 9 and 16, 1910; November 17 and December 29, 1910; January 19, March 2, May 11 and 18, 1911

2. *Word & Way*, July 7, 1910. 10.

3. Marks' Remarks, June 4, 14-17, 20, July 5 and 7, August 7, 16-17, 30, October 16-18, 31 and November 30, 1910.

4. Marks' Remarks, July 28 and August 4, 1909 and June 6, 1910.

5. *Word & Way*, November 1, 1910.

6. Marks' diaries, June 7-8, 1909.

7. Marks' diaries, April 19-25, 1909.

8. Marks' diaries, April 19-25, 1909; Robert L. Ross, *The Two Became One* (Master Design Ministries, 2005) 17, 67 and 80-81; L. W. Marks, "Ten Years of Effort and Achievement," in Reports BGCO, 1910; *Baptist Milestones in Oklahoma* 34-35.

9. Marks' diaries, September 21-22, 1909.

10. Marks' diaries, September 21-22, 1909.

11. Marks' diaries, July 15, September 15 and October 12, 1910.

12. Marks' diaries, October 12 and November 14, 1910.

13. Marks' diaries, November 22 and 23, 1910.

14. Reports BGCO 1911, 43 and 72-73.

15. Ibid; Marks' diaries, November 11 and 14, 1911

16. *Word & Way*, November 17, 1910 and January 4, 1912.

17. Marks' Remarks, January 4, 1912.

18. *Baptist Messenger*, October 29, 1913 and March 2, 1914.

19. *Baptist Messenger*, September 11, 1912 and December 17, 1913; Marks' diaries, May 25, 1913 and November 4 and 12, 1913.

20. *The Two Became One* 81; Baptist Gaskin. *Baptist Milestones in Oklahoma* 271-272 and 275-276.

21. L. W. Marks' correspondence April to August 1909, passim, Marks Collection and Marks' diaries, December 31, 1909 and January 5 and 8, 1910.

22. Marks' diaries, November 11, 1909; January 8-9, March 12, April 3, June 12, July 10 and August 3, 1910.

23. Marks' diaries, January 22 and June 3, 1911; Marks' Remarks, May 3, 1911.

24. Marks' diaries, August 28 and 29, 1911; *Baptist Milestones in Oklahoma* 130-131.

25. Marks' diaries, July 31, 1911.

26. Marks' diaries, August 8 and 28-29, 1911.

27. Reports BGCO, 1909 and 1910; *Baptist Milestones in Oklahoma* 52-53; Marks' diaries, September 28, 1909.

28. Ibid.

29. *Baptist Milestones in Oklahoma* 58-63; *The Two Became One* 20, 70-72 and 268-272; Reports BGCO, 1907

30. Ibid.

31. Marks' Remarks, January 5, March 23, April 23, May 18, and October 19, 1911; Marks' diaries, December 20, 1910 and February 10 and 22, 1911.

32. Undated, untitled typescript, Sermon Files, Marks Collection.

33. Marks' Remarks, December 29, 1910 and January 5, 1911; Marks' diaries, February 2-8, and March 13-17, 1911.

34. Marks' diaries, May 5, 1911; Marks' Remarks, March 23, 1911.

35. Marks' diaries, May 5, 1911; Marks' Remarks, March 23, 1911; and June 6-9, 1911.

36. Reports BGCO 1911; Marks' Remarks, September 28, 1911; Marks' diaries, September 12, 18, 23, October 25, November 1 and December 18, 1911 and January 1-6, 1912.

37. *Baptist Milestones in Oklahoma* 62-63; Marks' diaries, May 14-20, June 4-5, 1911.

38. BGCO Reports, 1912; *Baptist Messenger*, July 17, 1912.

39. Marks' diaries, July 30, November 7, and December 19, 1912; *Baptist Messenger*, August 13, 1913.

CHAPTER 6

Pastor, Historian, Businessman, Church Member

Marks spent most of 1911 searching for a full-time pastorate. He received some interest from various congregations in Oklahoma City, Blackwell, and other larger towns but began to focus his hopes on Edmond by the end of the summer. The church there had fallen on hard times with three pastors in the time since he had left. These were: W. N. Wallace, J. W. Willis, and L. L. Sanders. Financial struggles seem to have been the primary problem, but there were divisions as well, including continuing debates about parsonage issues. For instance, in September 1908, the treasurer reported that the church was $48.00 behind on Rev. Wallace's salary; Wallace resigned later that month. Then the church split 22 to 12 on the call of his replacement with the minority refusing to agree to make his call unanimous.[1]

Marks knew of that history and other similar events because of regular contact with members during 1911. He first heard of the Sanders departure in January, but his real hope was stirred by a visit with two women from the congregation at an associational meeting in August. They reported interest in his return, and he was stirred by their appeal. A letter from one of the deacons the next month indicated that the church wanted him back to "bring them together again." That letter was followed by yet others indicating continuing interest in his return but also reporting difficulties with financial arrangements. He finally was invited in view of a call in mid November. The church then responded with an offer of $700 yearly in hopes of receiving a $400 annual subsidy from the American Baptist Home Mission Society. They also explicitly authorized him to take time to earn additional income, and he quickly agreed to that arrangement.[2]

In some respects, Marks' return to Edmond seems as problematic as his resumption of work with *Word & Way*. He had left there only five years before because of the kind of financial problems and divisions that they faced as he returned. In fact, the financial problems were even worse. The church debt stood at $142.00, with yet more owed on the parsonage which was not suitable for residence.[3]

The simplest answer to the question of why he returned is Marks believed that God was leading him to do so. He believed he could unify them and lead them toward financial solutions. Those convictions were matched by his commitment to Edmond. In announcing his new position in *Word & Way*, he noted that he had always thought of the town as the best location in Oklahoma. The availability of the Normal School for his children and access to Oklahoma City, state Baptist offices, and the remaining *Word & Way* business there were other advantages as well.

His continuing writing with *Word & Way* and growing insurance business and other efforts also meant he would not be wholly reliant for income from the church. But, there was more in his decision than such practical concerns. L. W. thought of Edmond as home. On three different occasions before the end of the year, he wrote about how good it was to be home. Some of that sentiment was his relief about the end of heavy pressure for travel, but this was also the year he reflected on a small

Christmas pounding, grateful for the "small gifts from his people."[4]

At least some of his hopes proved justified during the next two years. The small Christmas gifts given the Marks' family were more than made up for by the donation of one member. He allowed the Marks' family to move to a house he owned and live in it free for the year. The house had seven rooms with gas and electricity. L. W. noted, "I will surely accept." His gift also included a hog. That gift was especially helpful as Marks was about to lose his Oklahoma City property, and the prospect of free rent allowed him to borrow the money needed to hold that property until it could be sold. That solution did not end all of his monetary woes, but he generated significant income from his business efforts in each of the next two years. He reported total income of $1,289.93 for 1911; the next year $1,539.09, and $2,135.77 for 1913.[5]

He also managed to spur significant growth at the church. That achievement was based on a restoration of harmony and other results from his leadership and his focus on visitation. Other gains could have been related to his typical directness. Sermons for January included the topics: "What kind of a pastor do you want" and "What kind of church I would like to have." By that time, he was already reporting new people in attendance and the successful beginning of an "old folks" class. Sunday school attendance reached 90 the third Sunday in January, 100 the next week, and that number became the new standard during the next few months, reaching 107 in April. Increased attendance soon produced membership gains with at least eight new members added by letter or statement in February. Another new membership was added along with five by baptism in April.[6] He reported some kicking about the adoption of new Sunday school literature but he supported that innovation.

In February, the church learned that they would receive only $300 in support for the year through the end of September from the Home Mission Society. Marks fretted briefly about the projected shortfall but assured himself, "The Lord will help me." In March, his hopes were justified when Amarillo Life Insurance Company made him "a fine offer." The church was already falling behind on his salary by this time, but the insurance offer permitted him to forego the subsidy. Business gains would also partly offset continuing budget and salary shortfalls at the church as the year progressed.[7]

Growth continued as seen in 22 additions in September and a record of 119 in attendance the next month. That pattern persisted through the next year. Attendance reached 142 in June 1913; some of that number may have gathered as anticipation grew for the annual picnic two weeks later, but L. W. reported similar members on many occasions in the next few months. That included a report of the "best" Sunday school ever in October, though he did not give the numbers in attendance.[8]

Other highlights give every indication that the church was flourishing and L. W. was especially delighted with growth of the BYPU and results from his mentoring of Fred McCauley, who was defining the skills and commitments that would make him a leader among Oklahoma Baptists and eventually director of the Southern Baptist Convention tent-maker program. L.W. would later claim as McCauley "his son in love and son in the faith" and the young man actually became part of the extended Marks family when Luther married his sister. For L.W., however, McCauley must have seemed to represent an extension of his own ministry and influence. That was especially important to L.W. for another reason as only Luther and Marion among his children ever assumed positions of church leadership in their adult lives. By 1912, McCauley had already emerged as a key figure in state BYPU work, following his introduction to that program during L. W.'s first tenure at Edmond.

Marks was delighted to find McCauley had returned to Edmond, where he was attending the normal school and working as secretary to the college president. L.W. then began to work with him closely in promoting the BYPU at Edmond and the state. In the fall, 1912 Marks and McCauley took a group from the church by railroad to participate at a massive rally of young people at Capitol Hill. McCauley then accompanied his mentor to the state convention later that year.[1]

The following April, the *Baptist Messenger* reported thirty-six messengers from eighteen churches on this "first annual" B.Y.P.U. convention, noting that Edmond had the largest delegation there. Besides a number of well-received speeches by Stalcup, Moorer, and Stealey, the convention passed a number of resolutions including one that called for "hearty cooperation with all good people everywhere along all lines of civic righteousness." A lighter note came when the young women responded to the fact they were in the majority in attendance but gained no offices or committee appointments. They renamed the convention a "Boys Young People's Union" and proposed to build a "Girls Young People's Union." They then proceeded to decorate all the officers with pennants inscribed G.Y.P.U. which the men wore obediently for the rest of the session.

The next month, Stealey filled the pulpit at Edmond. He complimented the church for having the "banner union of the state" and McCauley for his outreach efforts at the Normal School. The Edmond BYPU listed 110 members, including adults, with about 30 associates in 1912. The next year it claimed 122 members. Adult members included L.W. and Sadie as well as W.D. Moorer and other church members. Luther, Frances and Zulah were the only other members from the Marks family as most of the remainder were too young for membership. Other members included Rosalie Mills (Appleby) who would go on to become the first missionary dedication from the Falls Creek Assembly.[10]

By this time, McCauley was also emerging as a leader among those calling for the creation of a summer assembly, an idea that would come to fruition within a few years in the creation of Falls Creek Baptist Assembly. That idea had been born at a Sulphur encampment a few years earlier and gained more interest from frequent BYPU camp meetings. These developments preceded those reported in histories of Falls Creek. Later in 1914, Marks was pleased to recommend McCauley's being licensed to preach by First Baptist Church Edmond.[11]

Other bright notes from 1913 included the annual picnic, the organization of a Sunbeam band, and the church's hosting a citywide meeting on the "boy problem" in response to a growing concern about juvenile delinquency as also seen in a concerted YMCA drive at the time. Less significant was L. W.'s winning a Victrola but he reported that the "folks were pleased" when he played it during one Sunday evening service.[12]

The best news yet came as 1913 drew to a close. After deleting about one-hundred "lost, strayed, or stolen" members, the church was still able to claim 195 members. Finances, however, remained problematic, and that issue was coming to a head. L. W. had preached on the issue in November and was soon greeted with reports of grumbling across the church. Then, the finance committee indicated that a member canvas had documented so much dissatisfaction, it would be best for him to resign. L. W. was both surprised and puzzled but soon noted that the reporting from the canvas was nonsense and that the deacons had misjudged the situation.[13]

That assessment preceded the December business meeting and was confirmed when a large crowd then attended the meeting to head off any move to oust him. The finance committee's report the next week called for his continuation at the present salary and the adoption of a unified budget, eliminating special collections and assessments, an act Marks approved. The year ended, however, with yet another note about problems with the finance committee. Then on January 11, the church voted the new budget down, and he began to consider resigning, indicating he would do so unless the church approved a salary of $650 annually. With their refusal to offer that amount, he tendered his resignation on January 18.[14]

Marks never offered an explanation for what had gone wrong, but there are two likely explanations for the church's action. First and foremost, monetary matters remained a sensitive issue among Baptists of this era, especially when they were financially strapped otherwise as most of the Edmond congregation were. L. W.'s first report of any dissension came after his first reported sermon on tithing.[15]

That message came only after regular failure to meet his salary and was part of a series that also addressed the cultivation of prayer life, daily Bible reading, regular church attendance, and other spiritual disciplines. In that context, Marks was clearly addressing concerns much larger than money matters. But, the money topic was the one most likely to engender a negative response. Bible reading and prayer were private practices that all agreed were scriptural, that many already practiced, and others could ignore with little public consequence. On the other hand, tithing was both a new and suspect teaching for many Baptists, and it required a public response. Even the relatively anonymous pledge cards were often understood as contracts, and individuals could be called on if they fell short of the level of giving they had promised. Ironically, the *Baptist Messenger* recognized Edmond's success in the area of systematic giving just as it seemed to spur an anti-Marks movement within the church. The money problem probably was also exacerbated by the same one Marks had confronted with payments from *Word & Way*. The church members knew he had outside income, and many were averse to increase their own giving in order to add to the salary of one who already had some income.[16]

Second, as at Lamar, Marks' political activities may have alienated some in his congregation. He reported no political or other city involvement during 1912 but then met with a group in January 1913 to organize a petition drive to get pool halls out of town. They gathered ninety signatures that day, and he made no other references to the campaign, but that question was soon added to issues to be considered in an election in April.[17]

In March, Mr. (G.H.?) Fink, a representative of the group that had sponsored the petition requested that L. W. consider filing for mayor on the Democratic slate. Marks checked with the church finance committee and then agreed to run with the understanding that he would not campaign. That limitation was fairly common during the era and was meant to define a position above the usual political practices. The practice was linked to the famous 1884 declaration of William Tecumseh Sherman who had declined both nomination and willingness to serve if elected. At the same time, it also meant L.W. would have less risk of alienating church members. His effort to avoid confrontation was also seen when he acknowledged that his Republican opponent, the incumbent William Potts, was a good man, and it would be fine with him if Potts were elected.[18]

L. W. won by a margin of seventeen votes in April; none of the city council candidates he had mentioned were elected, but prohibition on pool halls passed by a resounding vote of 244 to 94. His election immediately added to his work load. The council met every two weeks with meetings frequently running to as much as four hours. His duties also called on him to preside as a Justice of the Peace in city court actions, and other city business demanded more of his time.[19]

These changes seemed to affect his business travel more than his church work but could have produced concerns among church members. Similarly, disagreements could have arisen over council issues. However, most city business involved routine processing of claims, citizen concerns about city services, etc. Even when issues troubled the council, they did not seem to draw much concern from citizens. For instance, the most contentious and long-lasting issue facing the council during Marks' time in city government concerned the possible relocation of the bell located on top of city hall used for calling the voluntary fire department.

The council first discussed this issue at its two regular meetings in June 1913. In September, the committee reported a recommendation to remove the bell and place it on a tower. The council split on the issue, and Marks broke the tie, so it did not pass. A motion to obtain cost estimates for a tower also lost. That was followed by defeat of another motion to have the superintendent of the city water and light plant draw plans for a tower to dry fire hoses. Two additional proposals to appoint a committee to remove the bell and contract for a tower for the bell and five hoses and another to create a committee to submit plans and ascertain costs for such a tower were also defeated. Seven months later, the council finally agreed to delegate the decision about the location of the bell to the superintendent of the water and light plant along with the responsibility for creating a plan for ringing it when needed.[20]

Such matters rarely drew the attention of the town's newspaper for obvious reasons, but the editor also ignored more controversial matters as well. He occasionally gave front page attention to varied matters from a decision to equip council chambers with coat and hat hangers to Marks' election and the pool hall proposition in 1913, but the bold headlines and more extensive treatments were reserved for news such as an announcement that Edmond was to begin receiving free mail delivery, effective April 15, 1913.[21]

Even in the climate of small town politics, the kinds of issues the council dealt with were not likely to lead to significant controversy, but there were two that may have had that effect with possible repercussions in the church. In September, the city attorney brought charges against the city marshal and his assistant for dereliction of duty. The council then agreed to dismiss the charges but to issue a reprimand to the officers. There is no record of a public issue resulting from the matter, but it may have been part of a larger community concern about enforcement of prohibition ordinances. In May, the council had dealt with the city attorney's refusal to prosecute bootleggers, and the council and their attorney seemed at odds on many other concerns during Mark's term as mayor.[22]

A second and more problematic issue arose from a dispute between the city and the Normal School. On July 11, Marks reported that President Charles Evans had not properly filed the Normal School water bills with the state. L. W. and a council member, Jim Moore, then traveled to Oklahoma City to meet with the State Board of Affairs about the schools' delinquent account. The matter simmered for the next month leading to the city's decision to cut off the supply of water to the school, leaving the president indignant and students and staff without water for a brief period.[23]

Marks and another council member met with Evans and then made another trip to the offices of the State Board of Affairs. At some point during the dispute, probably as early as the inception, Marks had argued that the city should furnish the water to the school without charge as he recognized the benefit the city gained from the school. Some council members were less willing to part with the revenue but finally managed to adopt a series of related measures addressing the Normal School situation.[24]

First, the city agreed to furnish electricity and water to the school, providing for a discount for electrical services if the bill was paid on schedule. The water contract called for the city to provide the first 200,000 gallons used each month by the college without charge and then charge the prevailing rate for all usage above that amount. Five of the eight council members supported this compromise, but subsequent developments necessitated a citywide election.

The election was held on September 15 and offered the voter two choices. A majority of the citizens supported spending $1,500 to drill a new water well with 160 favoring and 113 opposed. A larger majority endorsed the council's agreement with the Normal School with 179 in favor and only 95 opposed. A ruling by the city attorney then indicated that the election was improper. Then, the state attorney general issued a ruling upholding most of the city's action. That seemed to settle the matter for the time being, but a related problem would arise in 1921.[25]

Marks never offered an explanation for what happened at the church. He reported some personal sadness once his resignation took effect but focused on his hope that the church would do well. He began to work toward that end immediately despite a church action that he had to have regarded as a slap in the face. That took place when the church voted to offer his replacement $800 plus a parsonage. That salary exceeded Marks' request by $150. Nevertheless, he supported the new pastor, working with him closely in many areas. At the same time, C. P. Stealey told readers of the *Baptist Messenger*, Marks would be a "sympathetic and capable helper to any man" the church would secure as pastor.

Beyond supporting his new pastor, Marks responded to his new circumstances in a number of ways. Probably the most significant of these was his resumption of a manuscript on Oklahoma Baptist history. He had begun work on that project in 1911 with the encouragement of J. S. Murrow who also helped him gather pledges of financial support for the effort. He could not have hoped for a better sponsor or source of information.

Murrow had been a major figure in Baptist work for years, had participated in many of the more significant historical events and was a passionate advocate of the Indian's side of history. Highlights of Murrow's career included some of the earliest work among the Seminoles, decades working among the Choctaws, a founder of Bacone University and the Murrow Indian Orphans Home, editor of one of the state's first Baptist newspapers, an influence on congressional decisions to ban alcohol in Indian Territory, a facilitator of the first Baptist association in the state, participant in the first Baptist efforts among the plains Indians, and a promoter of Oklahoma Baptist unity. Ultimately, he founded at least fifteen churches, and ordained sixty ministers, most of whom were Native Americans. He was also known as the father of Oklahoma Masonry.[26]

Marks first reported on a visit with Murrow in April 1910. At that time, he commented only on Murrow's library and his fascination with the collection. These may have included some Masonic sources as Marks developed an interest in that organization about the same time, and that interest was likely due also to Murrow's encouragement. Marks did not actually join the Masons until 1914, but his contact with Murrow soon led to a project that would solidify his standing as the first chronicler of Oklahoma Baptist history.[27]

Murrow had almost certainly read Marks' biography of L. L. Smith and a historical report he had written for the 1910 BGCO entitled "Ten Years of Effort and Achievement." A little more than four pages in length, this report demonstrated L.W.'s growth as a historian and writer. He had not completely abandoned the didactic goals of seeking lessons from the past such as affirming "the guiding providence of God," or that Baptist workers had regularly rejoiced over successes reflecting God's abundant blessings on their work. In other respects, however, he would meet two standards of historical excellence. First, he managed to identify the key events and people who had shaped Baptist history in the state to that point. His outline could still be used profitably by any writer dealing with that decade.[28]

The second historical quality of the report was found in its interpretive strengths. He recognized that Baptist work in Oklahoma was built upon that of prior decades and linked to a larger national picture. He also faced problems honestly noting that the "faithful historian will record some things that bring a blush of shame." For Marks, these included "unbecoming continuations of opposing factions," perpetuation of strife rooted in the issues of the Civil War and its aftermath, confusion of "provincial customs and personal stubbornness for principles," and stress upon differences.[29]

The final sources of shame were the "catchy contentions of extreme Landmark and Gospel Mission brethren. Their persistent tinkering . . . drew off some brethren and prevented them from doing anything worthwhile. As they paraded the labor and expense involved in organized mission work, the lazy brethren approved, and the stingy brethren applauded." Their forces were offset by the "apostolic boldness and martyr sacrifices of the great body of Baptist peoples, . . . children of light" who mortgaged homes and sacrificed at meal times to build churches. In turn, such sacrifices and achievements allowed the growth of a body "cemented together in the fellowship of love and service of a common Lord . . . {with their hearts} set on the main cause, rather than incidental issues."[30]

His 1910 report is the only known occasion when he wrote in any detail about the history of the era he lived in. His contact with Murrow, however, eventually led to Marks' seminal study of Baptist work in Oklahoma prior to 1900. That study was intended originally to bring the history of the denomination up to 1910 but Marks was unable to complete a manuscript on the latter years. L. W. received a letter from Murrow on December 27, 1910, proposing such a study and Marks responded the next day. By December 30, Murrow and one other supporter had agreed to contribute $200 toward the history. At the same time, Marks drew attention to Murrow and his collection of books and documents through an article in *Word & Way*.[31]

By January, the list of supporters included Murrow, J. E. Linest, F. M. Overlees and Marks who each contracted to commit $200 to the publication and sale of the book. The amounts were to be paid in four installments beginning in February 1911 and ending in October. The withdrawal of one of the supporters before the first payment was due represented a "fearful knock" but did not prevent L. W.'s progress on the study. Murrow's money arrived as promised and others' probably did also, but the full support he expected never materialized, and he recorded no payments from any source after early 1911.[32]

He began study of secondary sources on Indian history in January that year and then began interviewing a wide variety of those who had participated in aspects of Baptist work in Indian Territory. Besides Murrow, he specifically mentioned A. J. Holt; John F. Brown, and his daughter Alice B. Brown, present and future governors of the Seminole nation; a daughter of Chief Charles Journeycake, A. M. Harjo, President Almon C. Bacone of Bacone Baptist College; and a daughter of Jesse Bushyhead, a Cherokee and missionary to his people. He also describes visits with tribal groups at the Wichita Indian association and writing a number of pioneer missionaries and compilation of a considerable body of written material from Murrow, Bacone and other correspondents. The minutes he had collected previously from associational meetings were also useful.

He wrote the forward and completed an initial outline in January 1911, writing and researching as time permitted through June at which time he submitted his forward and chapter one to Murrow who soon approved the work to that point. Marks used a meeting with Murrow the next month to add to his notes about many missionaries and early church leaders. That accomplishment along with the cessation of payments for his work ended his writing for most of the next eighteen months. He only mentioned the history one time during 1912 before resuming a concentrated effort from January through the spring of 1913.[33]

His completed manuscript, the "Story of Oklahoma Baptists," contains 154 typewritten pages plus a four-page introduction. The typescript was transcribed from his notes by his daughter Zulah. As with his 1910 report to the convention, the manuscript is closer to historical writing standards of the era than those produced by most amateur historians. L. W. consciously attempted to define political and other contexts affecting the events he depicted while viewing all things from the "standpoint of true historian, rather than the partisan advocate." He even succeeded in establishing an interpretive framework that would be echoed by many academic historians in the future. This was seen in his assertion that "he who tells the true story of Oklahoma must . . . prepare to move in a new land and breathe another atmosphere under a different sky." His sympathetic portrayal of the Indian view of the state's history added yet other qualities. At the same time, his work is strongly didactic as L. W. believed such emphases were part of his interpretive responsibilities.[34]

The manuscript contains eleven chapters, collectively named "The Indians Home." The individual chapters are entitled: "The Coming of the Cherokees"; "Religious Work Among the Cherokees in Their Old Home"; "The Trail of Tears"; "The Creeks or Muskogees"; "Beginnings of Baptist Work in Indian Territory"; "Kingdom Builders, 1840-1860"; "Twenty Years of Sowing and Reaping, 1840-1860"; "Gathering the Fragments, 1860-1870"; "Missions Among Plains Indians, 1870-1880"; "Organization and Development, 1880-1890." He had also hoped originally to add a second volume, "The White Man's Paradise."[32]

The breadth of topics and decades he covers meant that he devoted only a few pages, sometimes even paragraphs to many topics. Nevertheless, he accomplished many of the goals he defined, and his study has been the foundation for every history of territorial Baptist work in Oklahoma written since that time. J. M. Gaskin who regularly acknowledged his use of the Marks' manuscript in writing at least three of his diverse books on Oklahoma Baptist history, rightly praised Marks as the "stackpole" for Oklahoma Baptist historians and "the one person who could best be called ""the father of Oklahoma Baptist History."

The manuscript, however, was not ready for publication. There is considerable evidence that he never edited the manuscript once it was typed as it contains a number of typographical errors and some instances where his meaning is unclear. It also needed some additions; for instance, he does not deal with the history of the Cherokee Treaty Party. Nevertheless, it offers much to an understanding of Oklahoma Baptist and tribal histories. Sadly, there is no evidence of any use of the history by scholars outside state Baptist circles. This omission is best explained by scholars' ignorance of the existence of the manuscripts.

The problems in the work are more than offset by other qualities of his work. It is the first study of its kind, and he describes numerous individuals and developments whose stories have been lost over time. His attention to the career of Joseph Islands among the Creeks during the antebellum persecution of Christians is one of many such stories. The significance he gives to Native American Baptist work among their people and other tribes supports his contention that native preachers such as Jesse Bushyhead, Islands, and others account for the ultimate Baptist domination of Christian work among the Indians of Oklahoma. The fact that much of the content is based upon first-hand interviews with participants or their family members adds significance to his accounts. J. F. Murrow's contribution to the manuscript alone mandates additional scholarly attention.[36]

Marks' writing also sets him apart from most of the others who wrote on aspects of tribal history in Oklahoma before the 1970s. His assessment of the United States' treatment of the Indians depicted whites as lawless elements in the Indian homelands who expected and received protection when Indians sought to protect themselves. "When the soldiers came, they made no inquiry as to the merits of the case—that was none of their business—they went after the Indians, slaughtering them right and left. Under these circumstances, the Indian . . . could take his choice: he could be butchered together with his women and children, or he could lay down his arms and sign away as much of his inheritance as the white man cared for at that time. Anyone who reads the history of the white man's dealings with the Indians will become nauseated . . . with the frequency of this pattern."[37]

Other examples illustrate that conclusion. Writing of the Choctaw removal, he focused on rigors of the five-hundred mile journey undertaken in winter with many of the women and children barefooted and often underfed, commenting that the "horror of the whole movement may be imagined." He did not show as much sympathy to plains Indians primarily because he did not write of about their journeys to Indian Territory or of the wars they fought but still noted that many of those tribes' complaints were justified.[38]

Even while taking a prophetic stance against such treatment, Marks also remembered his concerns as a historian. While describing the "disgraceful journey" of the 1838 Cherokee removal with its "unspeakable sufferings" and "horrible afflictions," he recognized that it was not a simple story. He depicted individual officers and soldiers as "generally as good to the victims as circumstances would permit" even as he pointed to a wider tragedy than the journey itself. A "trek under such circumstances, could not but result in unspeakable suffering. Back of them lay the long history of their noble nation, of which they were justly proud. Back there were their ruined homes and the graves of their fathers" along with their broken hearts and hopes for the future. [39]

The final chapter in *The Story of Oklahoma Baptists* only contains three pages. These were clearly intended to summarize the preceding section and introduce more extensive treatment of Baptist work during the territorial period in the projected "White Man's Paradise." However, there is no evidence to suggest that he ever wrote anything more on that or other aspects of state Baptist history. In one sense, this chapter marked the end of a phase in his life as well as his manuscript. Significantly, his last paragraphs include the language from the paper he had written at Southern Seminary, defining his progressive values. He depicted the fruitful labor from the territorial period as the product of "a general Baptist Convention embracing all the Baptists in Indian Territory; a school of higher learning [Bacone University] for the education of their sons and daughters, and a Baptist paper of general circulation [Murrow's *Indian Missionary*]. These forces had kept Indian Territory Baptists from being lopsided, wasting their resources as they conducted a guerilla warfare, only irritating and angering the enemy."[40]

L. W. looked at the manuscript one other time in 1915, but his increasing commitment to business and other concerns probably prevented the kind of concentrated effort he preferred. Moreover, the history had proven to be another disappointment among the many he had encountered. His history rightly stands at a seminal work for the state's Baptist history, adding to his recognition among Baptist historians, but that achievement was largely unrecognized in his life time and its full potential remains to be developed.

He would face yet other disappointments in his church-related efforts the next few years. His resignation as pastor at Edmond did not end either his preaching or his associational and other preaching ministries. He continued to supply area churches regularly during the next few years, especially those within the boundaries of the Central Association. For instance, during the two years following his resignation, he preached at Immanuel of Oklahoma City; Britton; Yukon; Guthrie; First, Oklahoma City; Washington Ave., Oklahoma City; Piedmont; Hopewell; and, the Lowrie church near Mulhall.[41]

He served half time on a temporary basis at Pleasant Valley from December 1914 until April 1915. That association produced yet another in what would become a series of humiliations after the salary matter at Edmond. L. W. evidently facilitated the church's search for another pastor and worked with one young candidate the church soon selected. He regarded that young man as weak and unprepared but "a good boy, whose ignorance and egotism is almost equal to what mine used to be," so he was not too critical. His toleration was challenged by the pastor's conduct at Marks' last meeting with the church. He made a lengthy appeal to the church to make an offering for Marks, pleading his large family and great neediness. Marks was humiliated by the plea and by the collection, "a handful of nickels."[42]

Yet another rejection came from the church at Lowrie. He began preaching there one time monthly and led them to commit to planning for their first permanent building. As a result, he was soon facilitating plans for that church's building even as he was spending evenings helping with the concrete work for a new building at First Baptist Church, Edmond. Then on December 5, the church extended a call to another man, so Marks withdrew his name. He reported ruefully that he got to see the frame for the new building the following day but would not see it any more.[43]

The combination of a series of such rejections could easily have discouraged even one as committed to the ministry as L. W. In reality, he never thought of either the Pleasant Valley or Lowrie congregations as long-term commitments. Although he never stated it clearly, his actions were more consistent with a long-term interest in strengthening smaller, struggling congregations as seen in numerous efforts such as ongoing assistance to a Crescent congregation developing church business procedures. This would also be seen in subsequent months' long commitments at Witcher and Waterloo. He would maintain similar practices in the following years until age began to limit the required travel.[44]

Marks' children almost surely saw his experiences differently. They would recall a succession of hard years defined by meals built around donated molasses or other gifts. They remembered their father's frequent absences, his constant scrambling to provide for them as well as their own times of need, and they could not have helped but resent his treatment. As with many preachers' children, they had witnessed the uglier aspects of churches. Those experience probably account for the fact that only two would maintain prominent roles in churches as adults. Yet, each retained other expressions of their family faith and related qualities; the "positive truths" L.W. advocated.and the example he modeled.[45]

Beyond his contributions at Edmond and among smaller congregations, L. W. Began work with a gospel team movement and maintained a prominent role in the Central Association. The gospel team was with a recently formed interdenominational group of men that included Baptists, Methodists, and other denominations. The teams were linked to a national movement that Marks credited to a "Doctor Summerville." He identified no other figures associated with the movement or gave any sense of the scope of its membership beyond central Oklahoma.

Marks' team consisted of Oklahoma County pastors and concerned laymen. They often reported as many as forty decisions at the different revivals they held. The members also held at least one meeting monthly through 1915 . These meetings permitted mutual encouragement, discussion of strategies, planning, and guest preachers. At other times, they might go as a group to area revival meetings. Beyond these meetings, the gospel team raised money and sponsored interdenominational rallies with team members such as L. W. rotating preaching times. Their meetings were held in churches, community buildings, and any other location from street corners to cattle pens where they could gather an audience. [46]

The number of meetings seems to have declined sharply the next year with Marks mentioning only one, but his involvement and the organization persisted at least until 1917.[47] It may have continued thereafter in Oklahoma or elsewhere but that year also marked the beginning of American involvement in the First World War, a development that would foster a major shift in American Christian denominations. Emergent fundamentalism would soon challenge the spirit of interdenominational cooperation reinvigorating many of the old Landmark arguments among Baptists.

Later, these forces could find abundant evidence for attacks on liberalism in churches as Presbyterians, Methodists, and other denominations recoiled from their endorsement of the war. That change frequently included a drift from prior emphases on conversion. It also meant increasing attention to the idealized national and international qualities embodied in President Woodrow Wilson's Fourteen Points, especially his call for the League of Nations. Also, by this time, many of the mainstream denominations began to back off from their support of prohibition, a primary issue separating Baptists from the denominational mainstream in Oklahoma during subsequent decades.

Even before these developments, Oklahoma Baptists had begun a shift away from cooperation with other denominations. Despite Stealey's early statements about grounds for cooperation, both the *Baptist Messenger* and state Baptist leaders of the era were slowly but surely withdrawing from joint efforts even when it might mean weakening their own churches. The clearest evidence of this trend was seen in the abandonment of dual alignment with the Northern and Southern Baptist Conventions. That action had found advocates as early as statehood but grew in strength after 1912.

In conjunction with the Southern Baptist Convention meeting at Oklahoma City, the *Baptist Messenger* devoted four pages of the July 13, 1912, edition to the issue, quoting other Baptist newspapers throughout the region. All sources supported the separation except the *Central Baptist* newspaper of Missouri. That editor asserted Missouri Baptists had retained dual alignment and found it worked without friction. He went on to note that Oklahoma had been settled by people from all parts of the country, and the plan seemed to be working well there as well. In contrast, *Word & Way* supported the idea of each state being aligned with only one convention to "simplify, clarify, and unify . . ."[48]

Marks was at the forefront of a small group of well-known Baptists in Oklahoma who opposed unification. Two weeks after the *Baptist Messenger* published the comments quoted above, Stealey published Marks' rejoinder, even permitting him the use of the "Marks' Remarks" column name. He defined the call for unification as an unfortunate move and questioned whether there was a general call from the people for that action. While stressing his own Southern identity, he argued that the people of the state were not necessarily Southern. He also asserted that Baptists were making good progress at present and that the slight problem of identity was more than compensated for by the benefits of cooperation. He believed the present arrangement was most likely to produce an "all around Baptist" with a denominational rather than a sectional view.[49]

His arguments may have helped to delay unification, but they could not stem the tide. Oklahoma had undergone a demographic shift with an influx of Southerners in the preceding decade, and a corresponding spread of cotton production and farm tenancy increased Southern cultural influences. Theological shifts among Northern Baptists provided grounds for increasing attacks on the Northern convention. The *Baptist Messenger's* attention to these concerns increased significantly during 1914, after two years of delayed action by the BGCO. These included frequent references to Shailer Matthews, an academic historian and dean of the divinity school at the University of Chicago. A lifelong Baptist, Matthews was a prominent defender of many Baptist traditions but also of modernism which he defined as the use of modern science to refine and defend the central values of an inherited orthodoxy to the modern world. His defense of the methods of modern science and opposition to enforcement of doctrines by discipline brought him into sharp conflict with those he defined as dogmatists. Stealey clearly belonged in that camp, characterizing Matthews' arguments as a "broken reed."[50]

Stalcup supported unification but was reluctant to abandon a beneficial arrangement too quickly. He alone among the convention leadership recognized the contribution of the $8,000 annual Home Mission Board appropriations subsidizing Oklahoma churches. In 1913, for instance, the *Baptist Messenger* reported that the great majority of Baptist churches in Oklahoma were still holding services one to two times monthly and true self sufficiency remained a distant hope for many. Likewise, Stalcup valued the history of long-term and congenial working relationships with the Northern board. But, there was actually little room for compromise on the question. Baptist opinion in Oklahoma was clearly shifting, and the Home Mission Board was also indicating reluctance to continue its support for the long term. The 1914 convention ended the debate, officially linking the BGCO only to the Southern Baptist Convention.[51]

With that action and earlier decisions affecting Baptist higher education and newspapers, the prohibition question settled and similar developments there were now few issues to draw Marks' attention to the state level. He remained as historical secretary and continued to compile historic associational minutes until 1921 but he wrote no new historical studies and his attendance at the state convention was sporadic thereafter. In contrast, he remained active in the Central Association and its successor organization the Oklahoma County Association until at least 1933.

Beginning in 1913, the association renewed its focus on evangelistic campaigns with the renewal of some level of prosperity in the state though budgets for that effort and others remained subject to regular shortfalls. The association's employment of L. L. Scott in December 1913 and the purchase of a tent for his meetings were both timely and effective. By this time, Scott had earned a growing reputation as "Scottie the Baptist," one of the most colorful and effective Oklahoma evangelists of the era. His work with the association would add to his renown. Marks had participated in the bricklayer-preacher's ordination in 1911 at Immanuel Church in Oklahoma City. As association treasurer, Marks often personally provided the financial stability Scottie needed. This included advances to the evangelist from his own money and a fund-raising campaign through the *Baptist Messenger* to obtain necessary funds to purchase the tent.[52]

Marks' use of his own funds to subsidize Scottie's ministry is especially noteworthy as he reported a sharp dip in income for 1914, and he carefully avoided any comments on Scottie's preaching. That almost certainly meant that he did not care for it. Scottie was best known for his colorful stories and illustrations, even his willingness to fight those who would prevent him from holding services. Those were not the characteristics Marks admired, but, as with Sid Williams almost twenty years before, he believed God was using the evangelist; for Marks that was what mattered most. During 1913, for instance, Scott held seventeen meetings producing 207 conversions even as he also served as part-time pastor at area churches.[53]

C. M Curb replaced Scottie as associational evangelist in 1917, and the association maintained the evangelistic outreach even as it began to increase its attention to varied issues of the era. Some of these were related to American participation in World War I as in resolutions supporting food conservation and others calling for increasing chaplains in the armed services and urging Baptist volunteers for this ministry. Yet another called for restriction on unscriptural divorces. Such actions, however, represented the exception rather than the rule except for continuing attention to prohibition.

Other than evangelism, the association worked primarily to strengthen local churches and to garner support for vital agencies and programs. Both of these reflected Marks' deepest commitments. As he had from the beginning of his work in Oklahoma, Marks offered a strong voice in support of the orphans' home. His continuing work at the associational level on behalf of the home added to his earlier service for that ministry and J. M. Gaskin's depiction of him as one of the key individuals that kept that institution afloat in its early years.[54]

L. W. remained active in that and other associational work until shortly before his death, serving as secretary or moderator on a regular basis along with frequent duties as treasurer. By 1920, he had gained status as elder statesman and was given the regular responsibility of introducing new pastors to the meetings. In 1926, the association acknowledged his long service which had included duties as clerk in nineteen of the association's preceding twenty-five years. [55]

His service to the First Baptist Church of Edmond also demonstrated the strength of his commitments. He worked closely with every pastor he ever had, working as a layman to advance the goals he had sought as pastor. In doing so, he demonstrated the qualities he had defined in his sermon on what a pastor should be able to expect from his members: treating as "a brother, not a hired hand"; respecting as a shepherd and confiding in him; offering financial support; and, participating thoughtfully and prayerfully in church business. The latter area along with his regular teaching made him a key figure in the continuing growth and maturation of the First Baptist Church of Edmond. Once he became a deacon, he asked for the privilege of moving the adoption of every building project the church would undertake during the rest of his life.[56]

His frequent service as church treasurer after 1917 added to his contributions in this arena. His work on a church building committee during 1915 illustrated the impact of his leadership. As pastor, he had brought the church to the point that the old facilities were no longer adequate for Sunday services. In August, a committee began to work on plans to build a new sanctuary at a cost of $4,500. Two members of the committee resisted, but project supporters eventually prevailed. The church then approved a recommendation to proceed with the committee plans then calling for the building to be twenty-five percent larger than first projected. Building commenced by October, but Marks was not finished helping; he spent hours after his regular work on at least five occasions during November helping to lay the concrete at the new building.[53]

By the second Sunday in December, the church began using the as yet unfurnished building. The first Sunday, there was no heat, so the congregation shivered through services and what Marks labeled a "good sermon." The building was finally dedicated in May 1917 with seats, lights, and every other feature "fine." Dr. F. M. McConnell, corresponding secretary of the BGCO, was among those who joined Pastor H. J. Ridings, S. M. Brown, and Marks featured on the program. Perhaps best yet, S. M. Brown had led a revival the preceding week and focused on financial responsibility and the building debt. At the dedication, Marks would report it had all been subscribed.[58]

Later that year, Marks moved that the church permit a two-week vacation for their pastor, probably the first such action ever and then supplied the pulpit during Ridings' absence. His business skills and willingness to work for diverse goals added yet more to the advance of the church. In short, he became the kind of member sought by every pastor and needed in every church. The climax for his decades of service in this arena would come in February 1941 when he moved the church proceed toward another new building.[59]

The work of the local church represented Marks' deepest commitments, but he continued service to his community through most of the rest of his life as well. He had a little more than one year of service remaining as mayor following his 1914 resignation at First Baptist Church. Principal achievements during that time included a number of actions toward general civic improvements such as passage of ordinances for rubbish disposal, removal of old buildings, and some of the first regulations affecting automobiles. The council also made arrangements to house young men who would otherwise serve as volunteer firemen and passed an ordinance prohibiting the selling or giving away of cigarettes. Marks also used his office to promote improved public health practices. He urged regular water testing of water from both city and private wells. The year closed with the council considering the impeachment of the city attorney for drunkenness.[60]

Business continued along similar lines until March 1915 and new city elections. Marks agreed to run for mayor again but once again declined to campaign. He evidently expected his record to stand on its own, but this time his strategy backfired. He was defeated by three votes, a result he attributed to the wets. He did not seek any public office in the next two city elections but was appointed to fill a vacant council position in August 1919, after another man resigned. He would remain on the council for the rest of that term and was elected thereafter until 1924. He frequently served as President of the Council during these years and was usually on committees for finance, for streets, alleys, and sewers, and designated one of three water commissioners.[61]

The vast majority of the city's business during this period was both routine and conducted without disagreement on the council. One exception to this rule took place in early 1922 when L. W. proposed a wage scale for workers on city projects. This would have paid thirty-five cents per hour to workers and $5.00 daily for a man and team, but that measure was defeated. A lower rate was adopted a few months later. Another exception to the routine business occurred in 1923 with a decision to employ an individual on commission to identify any taxes that had not been collected. Otherwise, the city's business consisted mostly of decisions affecting trash disposal, the water supply, and paving and maintenance of streets. Most of these improvements were funded with bonds, but these were usually approved by the citizens. [62]

The town's newspapers printed council minutes but rarely focused on city business. This was both understandable and shortsighted. The business that seemed routine both then and now was also directly related to the city's long-term interests. The City Council's support of increased tree planting, whitewashing trees and the better cities movement were important contributions to Edmond's continuing improvement. Streets, water, the location of utility lines, and similar issues were not exciting, but the council's action during these years kept Edmond among the better places to live in the state for that time and for years to come. Marks valued these achievements and took a great deal of satisfaction in his role bringing them to fruition.[63]

He also earned some satisfaction from his business. He would never join the truly prosperous but he certainly improved his and his family's lot in that endeavor. He had defined the outlines of his business in the proceeding years selling multi-line insurance policies and real estate. At first the business grew slowly in part because he spent a great deal of time and energy on a series of fruitless ventures.

The first of these involved speculation in the Ardmore oil field during 1916. That area was experiencing a major boom at the time, but Marks' investments proved more problematic than profitable. He helped form a company with an individual he identified only as Harrington who proved both unreliable and unscrupulous. The company eventually brought a well into production, but it soon flooded out. Another oil venture the next year at Edmond was also brought into production, but its returns were short lived. Speculation in Texas land that year and efforts to revitalize a lead and zinc mine south of Baxter Springs, Kansas in 1917 proved even less profitable.[64]

In contrast, selling insurance and real estate in Edmond was a continuing struggle, but one that produced steady gains until the Great Depression destroyed much of his progress. He described his business as "trying to sell hard stuff to poor buyers" but slowly built Marks and Son's Real Estate and Insurance into a business that would become a fixture in Edmond. It also allowed him to improve his finances considerably and make some provisions for his old age. He reported income of $1,472 and $2,572 in 1915 and 1916, and in 1917 even better.

This did not mean instant prosperity but certainly exceeded his best year as a pastor, and the salary paid most Oklahoma Baptist ministers at the time. In 1917, for example, the average salary for twenty-six ministers in the Central Association was $1,140. And, although he faced frequent problems collecting insurance premiums when they were due, collection for business proved much more reliable than it had with most churches he had served as pastor. That relative prosperity permitted him to purchase an automobile in 1918 and to even afford "a belated honeymoon" in 1936.[65]

Marks especially enjoyed another aspect of his role as a businessman. He was able to regularly employ Zulah, Luther, Paul, and Marion as well as Fred McCauley in various roles. He frequently reported that they or others of the children had spent a part of the day in the office. Fred McCauley proved the most effective salesman, and Luther would eventually assume full responsibility for the business maintaining it until his own retirement.[66] These benefits were not all tangible but were treasured by Marks and brought him a great deal of satisfaction in his later years. He had, however, to face one final test of his faith.

L. W. made occasional entries about the health of his children, but the urgency and frequency of entries about Zulah increased sharply after 1909. That November, he noted she had a "bad spell of rheumatism" that required the attention of a physician. Two weeks later, she still had not improved, but she finally began recovery during December. After another bout the next spring, he indicated she was "not well—not at all." He never gave another description of her illness, nor reported a diagnosis from the chiropractors they relied on for treatment.[67]

Over the next few years, a pattern developed with the onset of problems during winter and slow recovery by the end of the summer. In the spring 1911, he feared that she would not last the week but she then rallied. On occasion, her needs for care were such that the family brought in outside help from Aunt Ran, other family members or an occasional hired nurse. By 1914, her condition had become chronic but relatively stable. She then reached a crisis stage in December 1916 at which time L. W. began to think about her imminent death once more.[68]

That sad event took place on January 3, 1917. L. W.'s diary entry for that day described his and Sadie's time sitting with her. "She asked for Aunt Ran and then talked to each of her brothers and sisters telling them to 'be good.' The angels came at 3:20, and she went away with them." L. W. seemed to find some solace in arrangements for the funeral and the funeral service which was held in the home. He would carry the sympathy cards he received upon her death in his coat pocket until his death. He wrote of Zulah and her sisters all dressed in white to match the white casket, and that it was "good to know that Zulah was at rest and happy." He concluded that "The circle is broken. We will never be 12 again. May the Good Lord gather us in his good home above.".[69]

There was something else broken as well. The combination of Zulah's death with the disappointments of prior years seemed to be mirrored in his attention to his diaries. The daily entries describing dreams, hopes, and accomplishments and disappointments fell off dramatically during the rest of the year. His last entry for 1917 was on Christmas day when he reported that he missed Zulah and his son Paul who had joined the army. His last diary entry was a happy one a few months later when he described his enjoyment of eighteen smart, interesting, and noisy boys in his Sunday school class. He capped that day taking Sadie, his mother-in-law, and another woman for a ride in his car.[70]

The events of Marks' life and career may have led to his abandonment of his dreams and high hopes, but his Christian faith endured. He continued his life of active service to varied Baptist and community causes. In most ways, this represented little change in either his commitments or the direction of his work. Though no longer pastor, he served First Baptist Church of Edmond literally until the day of his death on January 10, 1943. teaching his Sunday school class that day.

Among the few personal effects that L. W. Marks left when he died was a stock certificate for 600 shares in the Southern Boy Gold Mining and Milling Co. with a par value of $300. He purchased the stock in early 1909 and shortly thereafter reported one confidant had assured him they looked like a good investment. They were not.

It does not require too much imagination to see that experience as a metaphor for much of his life: A Southern boy, son of gold-seeker, he sought a different kind of dream in a different kind of field. He hoped to shape a denomination, fostering the growth of agencies and institutions to counter Southern Baptist tendencies toward divisiveness and provincialism in mind and spirit. Neither of the principal agencies he promoted toward those ends came close to his goals.

Oklahoma Baptist College never gained statewide support of Baptists and was the first to die from among the many colleges Baptists established between the territorial period and 1911. *Word & Way* never gained a major foothold among Oklahoma Baptists who finally developed and sustained their own state newspaper. Sadly, during the editorship of C. A. Stealey and at other times, that newspaper was as likely to promote the "one-sided Baptists" Marks feared as it was to counter their influence.

His career could also be defined by its disappointments. He never held the pulpit of a major church and was ultimately unable to meet his family's needs as a minister. The business he established supported the family and continued under his son's ownership after his death. Yet, even it certainly did not fulfill the promise of Marks' progressive-fueled expectations.

The metaphor of the Southern Boy is consistent with that summary, but L. W. Marks would not have agreed with it. Instead, when he summarized his life, he emphasized the blessings he had enjoyed. Even when he mourned the loss of his daughter and faced the doubts triggered by that event, he began with an affirmation of faith: "My Lord is good, but I do not understand it." About 1934, he wrote a forty-eight line poem entitled "Thirty Years with the Same People," expressing his gratitude for those who had helped him throughout his life, defining his hope for eternity with his loved ones in heaven and affirming his belief that his Savior had been with him all the way. And, if he had been able to see the future, he would have rejoiced to see the continuation of his values within the generations that followed. Those can be summarized in the tradition of regular family "hug-fests" and at least six descendants directly involved in ministry and dozens as faithful church workers. Likewise, he would have appreciated knowing that his descendants and the city of Edmond honored his memory in 2004, naming a system of trails after him.[71]

Such themes were almost certainly among those Dr. M. E. Ramay addressed when he preached Marks' funeral message. Ramay based his message on I John 5 which affirms the victory that comes to those who believe that Jesus is Lord.[72] L. W. was undoubtedly familiar with those passages and Jesus' teachings that his kingdom would be characterized by giving the greatest honor to servants. When that truth is affirmed, the metaphor for L. W. Marks life changes significantly. His story then becomes that of a man whose ability and training far exceeded the rewards he obtained in life but who was pleased to serve his master in whatever role he was given. This writer believes L. W. Marks found his gold mine in that service long before he claimed the golden promises of heaven.

1. Marks' diaries, January 9, 1911; FBC Edmond, Minutes September 8 and 13 and November ?, 1908.

2. Marks' diaries, September 4, 5, and 17 and November 12, 1911.

3. Marks' diaries, December 7, 1911.

4. Marks' Remarks, November 30, 1911; Marks' diaries November 24 and December 3, 22, and 23, 1911.

5. Marks' diaries, December 15, 1911 and unpaged sections at end of diary for 1911.

6. Marks' diaries, January 21, 25, and 28, February 4 and April 7 and 8, 1912,

7. Marks' diaries, February 5 and April 20, 1911.

8. Marks' diaries, September 29, October 13, and November 14, 1912 and June 1, October 12 and 19, 1913.

9. Marks' diaries, September 29 and October 8, 1912, Marks Family files.

10. FBC Edmond BYPU membership directory and log, 19112-191

11. Marks' diaries, April 22, 1913, *Baptist Messenger*, April 30, 1913 and FBC Edmond Minutes August 6, 1914.

12. Marks' diaries, September 23 and 28, October 4-5 and 29, and November 9-13, 1913.

13. Marks' diaries, November 23 and 30 and December 2 and 12, 1913.

14. Marks' diaries, December 3 and 7, 1913 and January 11, 18, and 25, 1914.

15. Marks' diaries, November 28 and 30, 1913.

16. Marks' diaries, December 13, 1913; *Baptist Messenger*, December 24, 1913.

17. Marks' diaries, January 20, 1913.

18. Marks' diaries, March 7, 1913; Edmond Sun, April 3, 1913.

19. Marks' diaries, March 7, 1913; Edmond Sun, April 3, 1913.

20. Edmond City Council Minutes (hereinafter cited as Council Minutes), June 5 and 19, August 21, September 18, and October 2, 1913 and April 16, 1914.

21. *Edmond Sun*, April 2, 1913; Council Minutes, June 7, 1915.

22. Marks' diaries, September 4, 1913; Council Minutes, May 12 and September 4 and 8, 1913.

23. Marks' diaries, July 11 and 21 and August 22-23, 1913; Council Minutes, August 21, 1913.

24. Marks' diaries, July 11 and 21 and August 22-23, 1913; Council Minutes, August 21, 1913.

25. Council Minutes, October 2 and 16, 1913.

26. Andrea M. Martin, "Joseph Samuel Murrow," The Encylopedia of Oklahoma History and Culture, <http://digital library.ok state.edu/encyclopedia>; H. Glenn Jordan, "Joseph Samuel Murrow, The Man and His Times," unpublished Ph.D. dissertation (The University of Oklahoma, 1982) 235; *The Two Became One.*

27. Marks' diaries, June 5, 1914.

28. "Ten Years of Achievement," Reports BGCO, 1910 76-80.

29. Ibid.

30. Ibid.

31. Marks' diaries, December 27-31, 1910; Marks' Remarks, December 29, 1910.

32. Handwritten and typescript copies of agreement, January 10, 1911, Correspondence files, Marks Collection; Marks' diaries, December 27-31, 1910 and January 18-19 and February 9, 1911.

33. Marks' diaries, January 14 and 17-19, February 10 and 13-14, and August 17, 1911; Thurston Tyson to L. W. Marks, July 27, 1911, Correspondence files, Marks Collection.

34. L. W. Marks, *The Story of Oklahoma Baptists*, unpublished manuscript, 1913, Historical Writing files, Marks Collection.

35. *The Story of Oklahoma Baptists*, title page and passim.

36. *The Story of Oklahoma Baptists* 62.

37. *The Story of Oklahoma Baptists* 2.

38. *The Story of Oklahoma Baptists* 25, 30, and 144.

39. *The Story of Oklahoma Baptists* 25, 30, and 144.

40. *The Story of Oklahoma Baptists* 152-154.

41. Marks' diaries, February 22, April 29, June 4 and December 17, 1914.

42. Marks' diaries, April 10 and 11, 1915.

43. Marks' diaries, May 16, November 10, and December 5, 1915.

44. Marks' diaries, April 29, 1914 and July 29, 1915.

45. Wynona Marks Holmes and Ship Marks interview February 3, 1996 and assorted family correspondence, Marks family files.

46, Marks' diaries, January 26, March 15, April 15, May 4, 10 and 24, June 14 and 21, August 2, October 4, November 11 and 17 and December 13, 1915.

47. Marks' diaries, March 20, 1916 and March 19 and November 4, 1917.

48. *Baptist Messenger*, July 13, 1912: 4-7.

49. Marks' diaries, July 27, 1912.

50. Marks' diaries, April 8 and May 12, 1914; *Baptist Milestones in Oklahoma* 191; Shailer Mathews at <http://academic.brooklyn.cuny.history/dfq/amrl/matt.htm.>

51. *The Two Became One* 39; *Baptist Milestones in Oklahoma* 191-195; *Baptist Messenger,* February 12, 1913, November 12, 1913, and December 24, 1913.

52. Marks' diaries, January 1, 1911, February 2, September 1, 2, 22, and 25, October 5, 1914; *Baptist Messenger*, March 12, 1914; see also: Bertharee McCourtney, *Richer Than Oil* (Smith Printing Co., 1956); this is a biography of Scottie by his daughter, but she provides little in the way of dates or other specifics.

53. Marks' diaries, January 1, 1911, February 2, September 1, 2, 22, and 25, October 6, 1914; *Baptist Messenger*, March 12, 1914 and Richer Than Oil; This author grew up with tales about Scottie as told by my boyhood pastor Dr. John R. Daniel, who conducted many revivals with Scott. The story I remember best, however, is one my father W. H. Turner, told about Scottie's sermon at a revival meeting in Perkins, Oklahoma during the great depression. Scottie took one of the church's chairs, proclaimed it represented the devil and proceeded to destroy it in illustration of a sermon. Dad commented: "We needed that chair."

54. Central Association Reports, 1917, 1918 1920: and 1926 passim: J. M. Gaskin to Luther W. Marks II, August 16, 1977.

55. Central Association Reports , 1919, 1920, and 1926 passim.

56. Undated, untitled sermon, Sermon files, Marks Collection. .

57. Marks' diaries, August 16-17 and November 18, 19, 22, 23 and 25, 1915; it is possible that some of these entries refer to work starting at Lowrie church during the same time, but that work was not authorized until November 10

58. Marks' diaries, December 12 and 19, 1915 and May 6, 1917.

59. Marks' diaries, August 1, 9, and 26, 1917 and FBC Edmond minutes February 26, 1941.

60. Council Minutes, February 5, March 12, May 21, and August 20, 1914; Marks' diaries, October 15 and December 17, 1914; Edmond Sun, August 14 and 21, 1913.

61. Council Minutes, August 19 and 27, 1919 and 1912-24, passim; May 6, 1920, January 1 and December 12, 1922; and January 7, 1924.

62. Council Minutes, August 19 and 27, 1919 and 1912-24, passim; May 6, 1920; January 1, January 5 and March 4, . and December 12, 1922; January 7, 1924.

63. Ibid.

64. Marks' diaries, February 14, June 6, May-October, 1916 passim;; and March 16 and September 1, 1917.

65. Marks' diaries, end pages 1915-1917; Central Association Reports 1917; Mom and Pop to Luther W. Marks, II, postcard October 1936, Miscellaneous Correspondence files, Marks Collection.

66. Luther left a teaching position at Fairfax Oklahoma in 1928 to join the business and in hopes of eventually pursuing a medical degree. That hope ended with the Great Depression.

67. Marks' diaries, November 5, 15, 16, 20, and 22, 1909 and February 18 and April 10, 1910; Marks did not provide adequate information to determine the exact nature of Zulah's illness.

68. Marks' diaries, March 3, 6, 27- 30, April 26, May 5, 10, 12, 17, June 10, 14, and 23, 1911; November 24 and December 29-31, 1912; January 8-9, 21-26 and 29, March 21 and December 28, 1913; March 7-8, 1914; November 14, 1915; and February 7, November 26, December 12-13, 17, 20, 24, 26 and 31, 1916.

69. Marks' diaries, January 1-6, 1917.

70. Marks' diaries, December 25, 1917.

71. L. W. Marks, "Thirty Years with the Same People," Miscellaneous Writings, Marks Collection; Marks diaries April 26 1911.

72. FBC Edmond Pastor's Record, Vol. II, June 1943.

Alvin O. Turner holds the Ph. D. in history from Oklahoma State University and is emeritus dean of social sciences and humanities, and professor of history at East Central University. This is his sixth book. He has also written eight chapters in different books and more than forty articles and encyclopedia entries dealing with aspects of regional and Oklahoma history. Turner has served as contributing editor for four different versions of *The Rainbow Study Bible,* and published fiction, poetry, and book reviews in varied journals. His books include*: First Family: A Centennial History of the First Baptist Church* of *Oklahoma City,* which he co-authored with Bob Blackburn, and *Letters from the Dust Bowl,* a finalist for the non-fiction award from the Oklahoma Center for the Book and for the Oklahoma Reads Oklahoma Initiative.

Made in the USA
Charleston, SC
16 March 2016